Tap, Move, Shake

TURNING YOUR GAME IDEAS INTO IPHONE & IPAD APPS

TODD MOORE

D1380756

Tap, Move, Shake: Turning Your Game Ideas into iPhone & iPad Apps
by Todd Moore

Published by O'Reilly Media, Inc. 1005 Gravenstein Highway North, Sebastopol, CA 95472.

O'Reilly books may be purchased for educational, business, or sales promotional use. Online editions are also available for most titles (*http://my.safaribooksonline.com*). For more information, contact our corporate/institutional sales department: 800-998-9938 or *corporate@oreilly.com*.

Editors: Shawn Wallace and Brian Jepson **Cover Design:** Monica Kamsvaag
Production Editor: Jasmine Perez **Compositor:** Rebecca Demarest
Proofreader: Kiel Van Horn **Indexer:** Lucie Haskins

Printing History:
December 2011:   First Edition.

Revision History:
        2011-12-09   First release

See *http://oreilly.com/catalog/errata.csp?isbn=9781449303457* for release details.

ISBN: 978-1-449-30345-7

[M]

To Dad,

It all started with that TRS-80.

ABOUT THE AUTHOR..viii

FOREWORD..ix

PREFACE xi
Who Should Read This Book   xii
What You Will Learn   xiii
Conventions Used in This Book   xv
Using Code Examples   xv
Safari® Books Online   xvi
How to Contact Us   xvii

INTRODUCTION TO XCODE 1
Developer Registration   1
Installation   2
Xcode   4
Interface Builder   26
Connections   30
Game Logic   34

HELLO PONG 38
Project Creation   40
Laying Out the Game Pieces   43
Multi-touch   49
Animation   59
Collision   63
Scoring   65
Finishing Touches   69
Sounds   81

CONTENTS

GRAPHICS 88

Introduction	90
Bitmaps and Vectors	91
Image Formats	93
Retina Display	94
Creating Images for an Air Hockey Game	96
Application Integration	116
Build and Run	121

PHYSICS 122

Paddle Physics	123
Puck Physics	139

SOUNDS 158

What Is Sound?	159
Creating Sounds	163
Downloading Sounds	163
Recording Sounds	164
Editing Sounds	167

COMPUTER AI 172

Computer Player Menu	173
Computer Player	183
Computer Difficulty	205

APP STORE 212

Screenshots 213

Creating the Application Description and Keywords 216

Submitting Metadata to iTunes Connect 218

Archive and Submit 224

App Review 226

App Marketing and Sales 235

Conclusion 244

INDEX 246

Todd Moore founded TMSOFT to create unique smartphone applications and games. One of the few developers to have had two apps simultaneously in iTunes' Top 20 Paid Downloads, his most popular game, Card Counter, was featured by Engadget, the *Los Angeles Times*, and CNET TV. Todd's most popular application, White Noise, was featured by iTunes, *Health Magazine*, *The Washington Post*, *PC Magazine*, and Late Night with Jimmy Fallon.

Todd started his professional career as a student trainee for the CIA, and after graduating from Old Dominion University with a degree in computer science, he designed network security and cyber forensic products. Since then, he's had numerous appearances in front of audiences: everything from demonstrating how to crack a popular VoIP application at DEFCON 12 to competing on the NBC reality show *Treasure Hunters*.

With the first Apple][it was very important for me to have a manual that would lead others to success and learning right from the get-go, even if the user had no relevant experience. That's how we learn. We start entering code others wrote to see how it works and then over time we learn variations.

One of my skills has always been designing things with the absolute minimum amount of chips. Before starting Apple, I saw the game of Pong at a bowling alley and I thought it would be fun to try building it on my own. My version didn't have anything to do with Atari's, but I did do it at least a year before they came up with a home version of the game that worked with your TV.

All in all, I ended up with 28 chips for my Pong design. This was amazing because it was back in the days before microprocessors appeared. Every bit of the game had to be implemented in wires and small gates. There wasn't a software program that was loaded and executed, it was all hardwired.

I visited my teenage friend Steve Jobs, who was working at Atari, and showed it to a group of engineers there. And they loved it! Later on, Steve called me to say that Atari wanted to do another Pong-like game. Atari's founder Nolan Bushnell wanted me to do it because he knew how good I was at doing designs with the fewest possible chips. Nolan had been complaining that the Atari games were going higher and higher in chip count, approaching two hundred chips for a single game. He wanted them to be simpler. And he'd seen how good I was at that.

They wanted a one-player version of Pong, but with bricks that would bounce the ball back to the paddle. It was called Breakout, maybe you remember it? So not even thinking about it, I said, "Sure." Atari wanted it using the fewest chips possible and I was up for the challenge.

The whole game was implemented in four days and used only 45 chips.

The reason I like this book and agreed to write this foreword is because it carries a message I've been holding closely my whole life. It is about simplicity and sophistication. Doing more with less. This recently has become even more important with today's mobile devices like the Apple iPhone.

Engineers should strive to do things more perfectly than even they think is possible. Every tiny part or line of code has to have a reason, and the approach has to be direct, short and fast. We build small software and hardware components and group them into larger ones. We write tiny bits of code to turn things on and off. Nothing would be elegant or beautiful without the engineer really thinking it out—really thinking about how to create the best possible end result with the fewest number of components or lines of code.

We build upon and build upon and build upon, just like a painter would with colors or a composer would with musical notes. And it's this reach for perfection—this striving to put everything together, so perfectly, in a way no one has done before— that makes an engineer or anyone else a true artist.

—Steve Wozniak

The App Store is one of the most innovative ways for an indie developer to publish their ideas to the world. You have probably heard the stories of developers striking it rich from an iPhone game they created in their spare time. Money is certainly a good motivator and why many developers are racing to get their ideas published. Do you have the next big game idea? This book is the complete do-it-yourself guide for anyone wanting to make the journey from game idea to App Store.

I've never seen such a widespread interest in creating apps and games than right now. Everyone from full-time professionals to children with iPod touches will stop and ask me the same questions: You have games in the App Store?" "How long does it take to create them?" And the one I hear most, "Can someone like me do it?" It seems as though everybody is interested in creating games for this new platform, but most just don't know where to start.

My entry into app development began August of 2008 when I started working on BubblePop. It's a game where you have to quickly pop moving bubbles filled with random numbers, and you have to do it in the correct order. I wanted my first game to be simple enough to quickly teach myself the platform, but challenging enough so my friends who helped test it actually found it fun to play.

When I started, I had no knowledge of the Mac, Xcode, or Objective-C. I also only had nights and weekends to work on my game. At the time, there weren't any relevant books and what could be found online was more about creating apps for jailbroken iPhones and not the official iPhone SDK. Even though I had a lot of things to learn and a full-time job during the day, I was still able to finish my game in a week.

I plowed my way into the App Store through trial and error. Now it was time to wait. My account and game needed to be approved by Apple. It seemed to take forever. It was torture. The day finally came when all the contracts were approved and my game was given the green light. I felt like a kid on Christmas day. It was

an amazing feeling seeing my work published on iTunes and available for the world to purchase.

My goal for creating my first game wasn't to make a million dollars. It was to learn the platform, create a fun game for my iPhone, and hopefully make enough money to pay for the 24-inch iMac that I just bought. As it turns out, I ended up making much more than that—especially when two of my apps, White Noise and Card Counter, hit the big time. In February of 2009, they were both ranked in the Top 20 overall for paid apps. I felt like I won the lottery when the sales report showed I was making over 10 times my current job salary. This was the moment I decided that my fun little hobby should become my full-time job. I have been creating apps and games ever since. I hope you can do the same.

—Todd Moore

Who Should Read This Book

I have been approached by numerous people who have ideas for games but just don't know where to start. If you have the funds, you could hire a team of developers and artists to create your vision. I've found that experienced smartphone developers and graphic artists do not come cheap. As an indie developer, it is important to learn all the skills necessary to do it yourself and hire out only when necessary.

This book is catered to those who have some coding experience but have never developed for the iOS platform. Have you built applications that run on either the PC or Mac platforms? Are you doing server-side web development with ASP.NET, PHP, or Perl and want to try building native apps? Do you already know C or C++ but have no clue about Objective-C? Or do you just want to learn how to build an iPhone game as fast as possible? If you answered "yes" to any of those questions then keep reading. I'm writing this book as the guide I wish I had when I created my first game.

What You Will Learn

I want to teach you how to create a game that uses those aspects of the iPhone hardware that make it unique when compared to other platforms. Most games are typically controlled using a directional pad, analog joysticks, and various buttons. The iPhone and iPad give us a new form of input—Multi-touch. We can track up to 5 individual touches on the iPhone and iPod touch screens and up to 11 individual touches on the iPad. This opens up a whole new genre of games that previously did not exist. This is why you are going to learn right from the start how to handle multiple touches on the screen.

You will quickly build a two-player game that uses multi-touch—and the exciting part is that most of it can be written with about 20 lines of code! Granted, it will look like the 1972 game of Pong, which probably won't be exciting for you unless you grew up with Atari's Home Pong console like I did. It is worth noting that the same techniques used back then also apply today in terms of game elements.

Let's think about that for a second. What does one of the oldest games, Pong, have in common with a 3-D first-person shooter like Call of Duty: Modern Warfare? Graphically, not much, but the game elements are actually the same—you control a player, that player has a position within a defined world, there is a goal to accomplish, and a score to measure your progress. Whether you are racking up points hitting a ball with a paddle or fragging your friends in a 3-D immersive world, the overall game elements are still the same. This is why I will start with a very simple concept and show you how to develop a more modern game moving forward.

You will take the game to the next level with flashy graphics and realistic sound effects. I'll show you a few tricks of the trade that are usually known only by graphic artists and sound engineers. It is extremely important as an indie developer to learn these skills in order to save time and cut costs. That's why this book

has chapters dedicated toward creating graphics and sounds. I will show you how to make the game look and sound like a real game of air hockey.

As you develop and test the new game you might notice that looks can be deceiving as the game feels nothing like actual air hockey. The puck doesn't move like it's on a sheet of ice. The table surface has no friction. Striking the paddle against the puck produces incorrect angles and velocity. You are noticing things about the underlying physics of the game that need to be fixed. I'll show you how to apply the math you learned in school, and thought you'd never use, to make our air hockey game feel like it's the real thing.

The final addition to the game will be creating a single-player mode that allows you to play the computer. Computer AI can be the most complicated and important part of any single-player game and this book makes the process as painless as possible. The first step is creating an algorithm that gives the computer perfect, unbeatable play. Games would not be fun if you couldn't sometimes win, so we'll introduce a dumbness factor that will make the computer player appear more human and make occasional mistakes. Having a mechanism to scale back how smart the computer player is will in turn give you the ability to have multiple levels of difficultly, ranging from easy to impossible.

Once the game is complete, you'll learn how to prepare it for the App Store. You will write a marketing description, create compelling screenshots, and submit everything to Apple for approval.

Let the journey begin!

Conventions Used in This Book

The following typographical conventions are used in this book:

Italic

> Indicates new terms, URLs, email addresses, filenames, and file extensions.

`Constant width`

> Used for program listings, as well as within paragraphs to refer to program elements such as variable or function names, databases, data types, environment variables, statements, and keywords.

`Constant width bold`

> Shows commands or other text that should be typed literally by the user.

`Constant width italic`

> Shows text that should be replaced with user-supplied values or by values determined by context.

> This box signifies a tip, suggestion, general note, warning, or caution.

Using Code Examples

This book is here to help you get your job done. In general, you may use the code in this book in your programs and documentation. You do not need to contact us for permission unless you're reproducing a significant portion of the code. For example, writing a program that uses several chunks of code from this book does not require permission. Selling or distributing a CD-ROM of examples from

O'Reilly books does require permission. Answering a question by citing this book and quoting example code does not require permission. Incorporating a significant amount of example code from this book into your product's documentation does require permission.

We appreciate, but do not require, attribution. An attribution usually includes the title, author, publisher, and ISBN. For example: "*Tap, Move, Shake* by Todd Moore (O'Reilly). Copyright 2012 Todd Moore, 978-1-449-30345-7"

If you feel your use of code examples falls outside fair use or the permission given above, feel free to contact us at *permissions@oreilly.com.*

Safari® Books Online

Safari Books Online is an on-demand digital library that lets you easily search over 7,500 technology and creative reference books and videos to find the answers you need quickly.

With a subscription, you can read any page and watch any video from our library online. Read books on your cell phone and mobile devices. Access new titles before they are available for print, and get exclusive access to manuscripts in development and post feedback for the authors. Copy and paste code samples, organize your favorites, download chapters, bookmark key sections, create notes, print out pages, and benefit from tons of other time-saving features.

O'Reilly Media has uploaded this book to the Safari Books Online service. To have full digital access to this book and others on similar topics from O'Reilly and other publishers, sign up for free at *http://my.safaribooksonline.com.*

How to Contact Us

Please address comments and questions concerning this book to the publisher:

O'Reilly Media, Inc.
1005 Gravenstein Highway North
Sebastopol, CA 95472
800-998-9938 (in the United States or Canada)
707-829-0515 (international or local)
707-829-0104 (fax)

We have a web page for this book, where we list errata, examples, and any additional information. You can access this page at:

http://oreilly.com/catalog/0636920018414

To comment or ask technical questions about this book, send email to:

bookquestions@oreilly.com

For more information about our books, courses, conferences, and news, see our website at *http://www.oreilly.com*.

Find us on Facebook: *http://facebook.com/oreilly*

Follow us on Twitter: *http://twitter.com/oreillymedia*

Watch us on YouTube: *http://www.youtube.com/oreillymedia*

1

Introduction to Xcode

Developer Registration

The first step in creating and publishing your game to the App Store is registering as an Apple developer. Registration will get you access to technical resources and iOS developer tools. This part of the registration is free but if you want access to Xcode 4, which is used in this book, you will have to grab a copy from the developer website or Mac App Store. In order to publish apps in the App Store, you will need to be registered as a full iOS developer, which costs $99/yr.

Navigate your browser to *http://developer.apple.com/programs/register/* in order to start the registration process. You will be prompted to create a new Apple ID or use an existing one. The Apple ID allows you to access Apple information and resources, register for events, and even purchase music and apps from iTunes. Make sure that this is an email address you actively use, as Apple sends email verification and developer correspondence to this account. If you are registering a company, you should use a company email address as your Apple ID.

If you register a new Apple ID, then you will need to create a personal profile. The profile includes an email address and password that will become your Apple ID. You will be prompted for this information to access certain areas of the Apple Developer website. In addition, you will be required to fill out a professional profile, accept the legal agreement, and verify your email address.

Now that you have an Apple ID, you can purchase the iOS Dev Center program and download the latest version of Xcode.

Installation

Once Xcode has finished downloading and the image has been mounted, you can proceed to install. Double click on the installer package, agree to licensing terms, and specify where you want to install. Select a drive that has plenty of space (see Figure 1-1), as installation will require over 10 GB of disk space. If needed, you may need to clean up old downloads or empty the trash to free up some space.

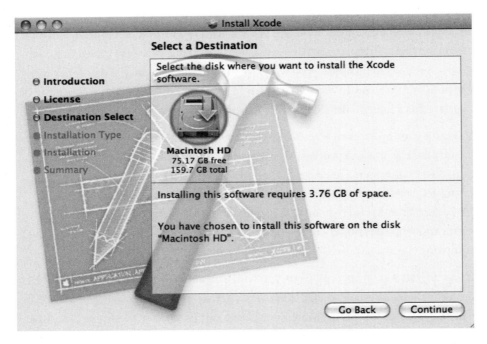

Figure 1-1. Select Disk to Install Xcode

After selecting the disk where you want to install Xcode, click Continue and go to the next screen. If you are installing a fresh copy of Xcode or upgrading from a previous version, you can just accept the default *Developer* location, as shown in Figure 1-2.

If you would like to have two different versions of Xcode installed, changing the location to something other than the default will allow for this. I typically will install beta versions of Xcode into a different folder but keep the most stable version in the *Developer* folder. For example, when Xcode 4 was still a developer preview, I specified the folder *DeveloperBeta* while keeping Xcode 3 in the default *Developer* directory. This strategy worked well and enabled me to work in both versions of Xcode.

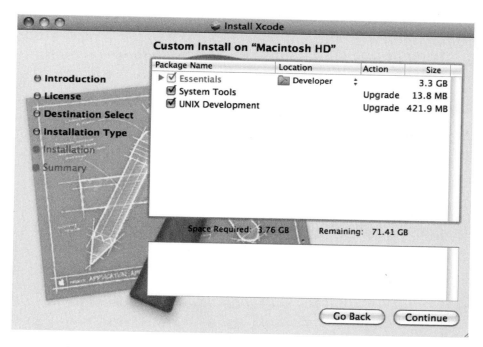

Figure 1-2. Selecting location to install Xcode

After clicking Continue you will proceed to the installation screen where you will click Install. Once the installation has started, it is a good time to go make a cup of coffee, as it will take a while to complete.

Xcode

Now that Xcode has been installed, we will take a tour and learn a few important features. Launch Xcode by navigating to the folder you specified for Xcode installation and then open the *Applications* subfolder where you will find the Xcode application. You should go ahead and drag it into your Dock so you can quickly launch it in the future.

In order to see the Xcode workspace, you will first need to create a new project. Either click on "Create a New Project" from the welcome splash screen, or select File→New→New Project from the menu. At this point you will be presented with numerous project templates (see Figure 1-3) that provide you a starting point for your new application.

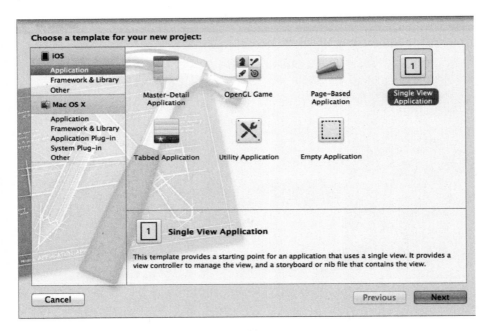

Figure 1-3. Xcode project types

Project Types

There are several project templates that you can choose from:

Page-based Application

> This includes a page view controller that displays items as pages, allowing you to navigate between items by turning pages.

OpenGL Game

> This template provides for an OpenGL ES-based view and a timer that animates the view. Games that use OpenGL ES as a starting point will require much more coding. If you want to use the powerful capabilities of OpenGL ES, you should look at using a library such as *cocos2d* (*http://www.cocos2d-iphone.org/*) versus starting with this template.

Master-Detail Application

> This is an iPad-specific template that uses the split view controller to display two independently controlled views on the screen. It is similar to the Mail application on iPad, which uses a split view controller to display a list of emails on the left side of the screen and the selected email in the main window area. It also supports all screen orientations.

Tabbed Application

> This template provides a Tab bar along the bottom and sets up a view controller for your first Tab bar item. The App Store application is implemented with a Tab bar that provides different ways to view apps in the store.

Utility Application

> This template demonstrates how to create two different views that can be flipped between. It sets up an Info button to flip the main view to the flip side view. The flip side view includes a navigation bar with a Done button to flip back. The iBooks application is similar in that you flip between your bookshelf and the iBooks Store.

Single View Application

This template provides a starting point for a single-view app. It includes a view controller to manage the view, and a nib file that contains the view. This is the template you will be using as the starting point for all the projects created in this book.

Empty Application

This is the most basic of all the templates, as it just contains a window and an application delegate.

Instead of doing a typical "Hello World" application, you are going to build a really simple game while taking a tour of Xcode. Select the Single View Application as your template, click Next, enter *Game* as the new name of the project, and then set your Class Prefix to Game as shown in Figure 1-4. Change the company identifier to either reflect your name, website, or company. Keep the device family set to iPhone. I will not be covering Storyboard, Automatic Reference Counting, or Unit Tests in this book, so leave those options deselected. Click Next, which will prompt you for a location to save the project (if you can't make up your mind where to put it, the Desktop is fine). You also have the option to enable source control by creating a local git repository. Although I will not be covering source control, I highly recommend enabling this feature if you do not already have a server set up. Click the Create button to generate your new Game project.

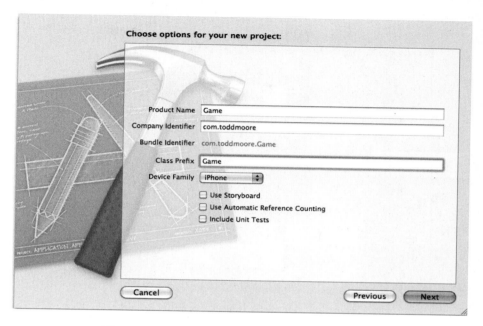

Figure 1-4. Creating the first project

Now that you have created a project, the Xcode main workspace window is displayed. If at any point you would like to get more information about a certain part of the interface, you can Control-click in a specific area and open up a help option from the menu. We will now explore how to navigate around the Xcode interface.

Xcode Interface

The Xcode interface is divided into four areas: Navigator, Editor, Utility, and Debug (see Figure 1-5). In order to display all the navigation areas, you will need to enable them from the View selector located on the right side of the toolbar. The View selector contains three toggle buttons that either hide or show the Navigator (on by default), Debug, or Utility Areas. The View menu can also be used to show or hide the different areas.

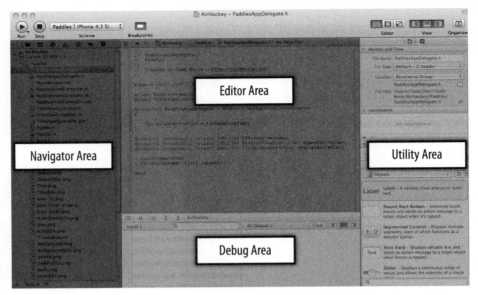

Figure 1-5. Xcode workspace window

Navigator Area

The Navigator Area is located on the left side of Xcode and allows for project navigation in many different ways. The navigator selector bar along the top of this area allows you to change between the different navigators: Project, Symbol, Search, Issue, Debug, Breakpoint, and Log. Selecting items listed in any of the navigators will open the associated file in the Editor Area. Along the bottom is the filter bar, which displays additional operations such as filtering and searching against the currently selected navigator. The filter bar will change to reflect the operations that the currently selected navigator supports.

The Project navigator, which is shown by default, displays the contents of a project as a list of groups (represented by folder icons) and files. This will probably be your most used view, as it quickly lets you find and open everything used to build your project, including source code and interface files. You may notice it also displays a list of Frameworks that your project is linking against. The filter bar at the bottom of the Project navigator lets you add new files (plus icon) to your project. It supports different filters, such as showing only recently edited files, files with source control status, and files with unsaved changes. In addition there is a search field you can use for keyword searches over the filenames (not the content) included in the view. For example, if you search for "view," you will see every filename that contains that word, including the *GameViewController.h*, *GameViewController.m*, and *GameViewController.xib* files.

The Symbol navigator lets you browse all the symbols in your project, including classes, protocols, functions, structs, unions, enums, types, and globals. You can view the project symbols as either Hierarchical or Flat. The Hierarchical view will display the entire class hierarchy or inheritance path of every object, which usually means starting with **NSObject** and navigating down. The Flat view will display each symbol without the hierarchy so every symbol is displayed in a single list. The Flat view is my preferred way of viewing classes, as it makes it easy to quickly locate a symbol. The filter bar supports showing class symbols only (filter everything but class names, including functions, structs, and globals), project-defined symbols only (filter framework classes such as **NSString**), containers only (hides class methods and variables), and showing symbols with a matching name typed into the search bar. All the listings are sorted alphabetically, which makes it easy to quickly locate methods of a specific class. As such, you may find it useful to enable the class and project symbol filters while leaving the container filter disabled.

The Search navigator lets you find specific text that is contained in any of the project files. Every resulting keyword that matches will be added to the list. The filter bar allows you to filter the search results displayed in the list.

The Issue navigator will display errors and warnings that are generated in the project. Issues can be displayed while you are editing source code or from building the project. They can also be categorized either by file or type of issue. The filter bar supports displaying issues from the latest build only, from the current scheme, showing errors only, and showing issues with matching content.

The Debug navigator is used during the debug of your application, along with the debug area, which we will discuss a little later. By default, the Debug navigator is opened whenever you pause the application or the debugger hits a breakpoint. Each thread in the application and its associated stack frames are visible within this view. The filter bar allows for showing just threads that have crashed or that contain debug symbols. It also includes a slider to control how much of the thread stack is displayed.

The Breakpoint navigator displays all the active and inactive breakpoints that have been added to the project. The filter bar allows you to add a symbolic or exception breakpoint, delete existing breakpoints, show active breakpoints only, and show breakpoints with matching content specified in the search bar. If you Control-click on the project icon, you can disable or delete all breakpoints in the entire project.

The Log navigator displays logs that Xcode created during project activities such as build, debug, and source-control tasks. The filter bar lets you display only recent logs or show logs with a matching name specified in the search bar.

Editor Area

The Editor Area is located in the center of the Xcode workspace and is the place where you will be spending most of your time. The Editor supports modification of many types of data, including source code, property lists (*.plist* files), and user interface (*.xib*) files. The Editor includes features that will aid you in writing source code, such as Code Completion and Fix-it suggestions.

You can bring up Code Completion (Figure 1-6) by pressing Control-space bar whenever you need suggestions on symbol names. Dismiss Code Completion by pressing Control-space bar again. Navigate the suggestions list by using the up and down arrow keys. Press Return when you want to use a symbol suggestion, and if there are parameters to a method name, you can press Tab to fill in each one.

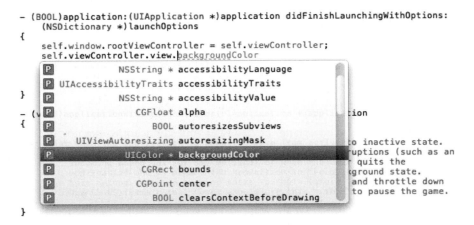

Figure 1-6. Xcode code completion

Fix-it (Figure 1-7) scans your source code as you type and marks syntax errors with a red underbar or a caret at the error location. Clicking on the symbol will display a message about the syntax error and in some cases offer a fix. If a fix is offered, you can select the correction and press Return to accept it. Pressing Esc will cancel the operation.

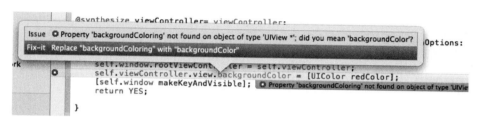

Figure 1-7. Xcode Fix-it suggesting a correction

The use of Fix-it requires building the project with the LLVM compiler. This is the default for new projects. However, if you are opening a project created in a prior version of Xcode, you may need to change the compiler in the build settings. Fix-it also requires fully indexing the project before displaying syntax errors. Indexing will start automatically when you first open the project. This process runs in the background and may take a few minutes to complete.

The gutter and focus ribbon are vertical strips running down the left side of the Editor window. The gutter allows you to manage your breakpoints for debugging. Click in the gutter next to a line of source code and a breakpoint will be added at that location. If you click the breakpoint again it will change to inactive. See Figure 1-8 for examples of both active and inactive breakpoints in the gutter. To delete the breakpoint, Control-click on the breakpoint and select Delete Breakpoint from the pop up menu. The focus ribbon is located between the gutter and the editor. It is used to hide or show parts of source code. If you move the mouse pointer over the focus ribbon it will highlight portions of the code that you can fold. Clicking will then hide the code and represent it in the editor as an ellipsis button, shown at the bottom of Figure 1-8. Clicking in the focus ribbon next to the folded code will then make the code visible again. You can also double-click on the ellipsis button in the source code editor to unfold.

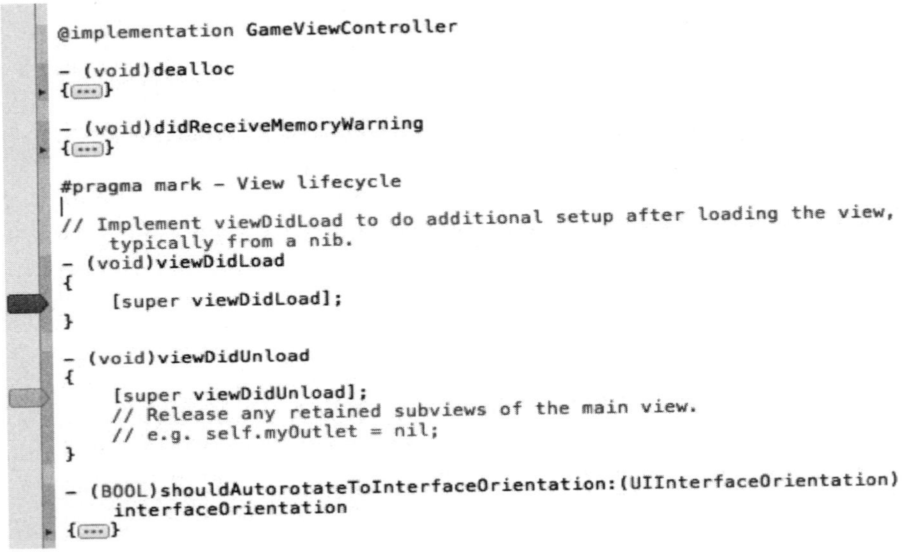

```objc
@implementation GameViewController

- (void)dealloc
{...}

- (void)didReceiveMemoryWarning
{...}

#pragma mark - View lifecycle

// Implement viewDidLoad to do additional setup after loading the view,
    typically from a nib.
- (void)viewDidLoad
{
    [super viewDidLoad];
}

- (void)viewDidUnload
{
    [super viewDidUnload];
    // Release any retained subviews of the main view.
    // e.g. self.myOutlet = nil;
}

- (BOOL)shouldAutorotateToInterfaceOrientation:(UIInterfaceOrientation)
    interfaceOrientation
{...}
```

Figure 1-8. Gutter showing breakpoints and folded source code

Utility Area

The Utility Area is used to supplement the information in the Editor Area. It is located on the right side of Xcode and provides access to various inspectors and libraries. Open up the *GameAppDelegate.h* file and make sure the Utilities view is shown. You can hide or show the Utilities Area by using the View selector in the toolbar, selecting View→Utilities→Show | Hide Utilities from the menu, or by pressing Option-Command-0. The File Inspector will now display information about the file itself, allowing you to rename it, change its file type, get full path information, modify localization, configure target membership, and modify text settings.

Just above the File Inspector is a pair of icons that let you switch between the File Inspector and Quick Help, which is extremely useful in displaying help information for items in the source editor. Placing the insertion point in an API symbol will display Quick Help information. Give it a try by placing the insertion point in the **UIApplicationDelegate** protocol of the *GameAppDelegate.h* file. Quick Help will display information about the **UIApplicationDelegate** and include links that will open to the full help documentation, as shown in Figure 1-9.

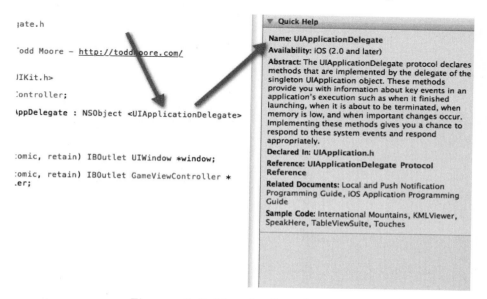

Figure 1-9. Xcode Quick Help

Debug Area

The Debug Area is located along the bottom of Xcode and will open automatically when you are running code or when the debugger stops at a breakpoint. This area allows for control of your program's execution while viewing variables and console output. The area is divided into three sections, with a debug bar along the top, variables on the left, and console output on the right. Although the view appears automatically, there are times when you may need to make the view visible (use View→Show Debug Area) such as when debugging has finished or when you want to view console output.

Building and Running

In order to build and run the application, you need to set the Scheme that you want to target. This can either be set to the Simulator or a device that you have registered for development.

Simulator

Make sure the Scheme, which is located next to the Run and Stop buttons in the toolbar, is set to iPhone Simulator. Clicking the Run button on the toolbar will build the application, install it in the Simulator, and run it (see Figure 1-10) with the debugger attached. You can also run the application by selecting Product→Run from the menu or by using the Command-R keyboard shortcut.

Congratulations! You just made your first application. Granted, it doesn't do much, but I've seen flashlight apps that didn't do much more. Now that the Simulator is up and running, let's go over a few common functions, as shown in Table 1-1, that you will find useful for testing applications.

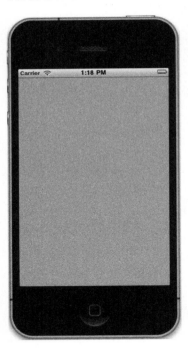

Figure 1-10.
Application running
in the Simulator

Table 1-1. Simulator operations

Menu operation	Description
Hardware→Device	Changes the Simulator between iPad, iPhone, and iPhone 4 (Retina display). These devices all have different resolutions, with iPad at 1024×768, iPhone at 320×480, and iPhone 4 at 640×960.
Hardware→Version	Changes the version of the current Simulator, which allows you to verify the application will run on older versions of iOS.
Hardware→Rotate Left | Right	Rotates the Simulator into one of the four orientations, including Portrait, Landscape Left, Landscape Right, and Upside Down Portrait.
Hardware→Shake Gesture	Simulates shaking the device.
Hardware→Home	Returns to the home screen from an active application. You can also press the home button on the Simulator window.
Hardware→Lock	This will enable the screen lock, which lets you test when your application goes inactive.
Hardware→Simulate Memory Warning	Simulates a memory warning, which can cause views in your code to be unloaded. It is extremely useful in testing if your application handles low memory conditions correctly.

Window→Scale	Reduces screen resolution to half the size. You can manually change the scale of the Simulator to 50%, 75%, or 100%.
iOS Simulator→Reset Content and Settings	Resets to factory default settings. If at any point your simulator becomes hung up or corrupted then this is your best option to fix it.

It is important to always test your application on an actual iOS device. The Simulator is just that, a simulation of the device. Nothing can replace running it on the actual hardware that people will be playing your game on. There are also limitations to what you can do within the Simulator, as it doesn't support the accelerometer or allow for true multi-touch. It is also beneficial to have devices that are not using latest generation hardware because performance can be much different between each generation. I test my apps and games on a lot of different devices and iOS versions, but the one that finds the most issues is my original iPhone running iOS 3.0. If you want to support all versions of iOS back to version 3.0, then an old iPhone is a great device to keep in your testing arsenal. Hopefully you already have an iPod touch, iPhone, or iPad that you can use for testing your applications on a device.

Device

In order to run the application on a device, you need to first connect the device to the Mac using the USB dock connector. Change the current scheme from iOS Simulator to iOS Device. Try running the application. If you have not already registered your device for development, you will get notified that there is no provisioned device available. If that is the case, open the Organizer application by clicking on the Organizer toolbar button on the far right side of the toolbar, or by clicking Window→Organizer from the menu. In the Organizer application, click the Devices tab, and make sure the connected device is selected in the Devices list. Click the Use for Development button (Figure 1-11) and wait until the device is initialized. You may be prompted to log in to your Apple Developer account so that the device can be registered and appropriate information downloaded.

Figure 1-11. Xcode Organizer registering new device for development

After the device has been successfully registered for development then you can close Organizer and return to Xcode. You should notice that the name of the device now appears in the current scheme.

Run the application and it will build, install, and run it on the connected device. The application can be debugged on device just like it can be in the Simulator. You will also notice when you quit the application that there is now an application icon on the SpringBoard (iOS home screen) just like you downloaded it from the App Store. You will now be able to launch the application on the device without having the dock cable attached. However, in order to debug and view console output from the app, you will need to leave the device connected with the dock connector.

Code Structure

Now that you know the layout of Xcode and are able to run the app in the Simulator and device, let's walk through the skeleton files that Xcode gave to you when you chose the Single View Application project template. Make sure the Project Navigator is selected in the Navigator Area and the groups are expanded to reveal all the files in the project. Click on each file listed in Table 1-2 to view the file contents in the editor window.

Table 1-2. Project files

Filename	Description
GameAppDelegate.h	Interface file for the application delegate, `GameAppDelegate`, which contains properties for the window (`UIWindow`) and view controller (`GameViewController`).
GameAppDelegate.m	Implementation file for the application delegate, `GameAppDelegate`, which implements the `didFinishLaunchingWithOptions` method to display the main window. There are numerous delegate methods that get called when the application changes to different states.
GameViewController.h	Interface file for the game view controller, which is assigned as root view controller for the main window.
GameViewController.m	Implementation file for the game view controller, which manages interactions with the interface. You will do most of your work in this file.
GameViewController.xib	User interface file (nib file) for the `GameViewController` view. You will work within this file to drop in UI controls and lay out the primary interface of the application.

Game-Info.plist	Application info file that specifies a lot of information about the application, including name, version, and which nib file to load for the main window.
InfoPlist.strings	This file can be used to specify localized versions of strings used in the application.
Game-Prefix.pch	Prefix header that speeds up overall build times by precompiling headers specified in this file. The contents of this file and the files it includes should rarely change, in order to speed up compilation.
main.m	Includes the main function that is implemented to set up memory management by creating an auto release pool. It then calls the `UIApplicationMain` function, which ultimately creates the main window and calls the application delegate. I have never modified the main function for iPhone or iPad apps, but in the case of Mac App Store applications, you might add license key checks here.

I will now explore how an application starts up so you can better understand how all of these files relate to each other.

Application States

I'll show you how an application starts up and goes through the different states by using the `NSLog` function. This function will log a message to the Apple System Log facility. It supports variable arguments similar to how the `printf` function works. These messages will appear in the Debug output window and are always logged regardless if running in Debug or Release builds of the application.

All programs start with a main function and iPhone apps are no different. Open up the *main.m* implementation file, which is usually located in the Supporting Files group in the Project Navigator. The implementation of the `main` function is pretty small as it only creates an `NSAutoreleasePool` and then calls the

UIApplicationMain function. The autorelease memory pool is used in the management of reference counted objects. You don't need to worry too much about its function, just know that it is needed to free some objects up when they are no longer needed. The **UIApplicationMain** function creates the application object, application delegate, and sets up the event cycle. Add a call to the **NSLog** function, which will report when the program is in the main function of the application. The main function should be modified to appear as follows (the line you must add is shown in bold):

```
int main(int argc, char *argv[])
{
    NSLog(@"main");
    @autoreleasepool
    {
        return UIApplicationMain(argc,
                                 argv,
                                 nil,
            NSStringFromClass([GameAppDelegate class]));
    }
```

The main function will now write to the debug window the message **"main"** as soon as the application starts. You are writing this message to show that the main function does in fact execute prior to any of the application delegate methods. I will investigate each of those methods next.

Open up the application delegate implementation by clicking on the *GameAppDelegate.m* file in the Project Navigator. A delegate is kept informed about the actions of another object. In the case of the application delegate, it is notified by the application when it goes into different application states. For example, the application delegate is notified when the application first launches as well as when it terminates or goes into the background. The different application states that the application delegate is notified about are listed in Table 1-3.

Table 1-3. Application state changes

`application:didFinish` `LaunchingWithOptions`	Notifies the delegate that the app has launched; this is usually the place to initialize application variables and data structures, read in application configuration, and decide which view will appear in the main window. If your application persists its state between launches, you should use this function to restore the application to the previous state.
`applicationDidBecome` `Active`	Notifies the delegate that the application has become active. This will be called any time your application moves from an inactive state to an active state, including when it is first launched. You should restart any tasks that were paused when the application went into an inactive state.
`applicationDid` `EnterBackground`	Notifies the delegate that the application is now in the background. In iOS 4.0 and later, this method is called instead of the `applicationWillTerminate` method when the user quits an application that supports background execution. Applications compiled for iOS 4.0 support quick switching, which just suspends your application and does not terminate. However, you should typically implement this function as if your application is about to terminate and save any state required. If the device is rebooted, the application will relaunch as a new process and not enter the foreground from a suspended state.
`applicationWillEnter` `Foreground`	Notifies the delegate that the application is about to enter the foreground. This is typically handled by restoring any tasks that were stopped when the app entered the background state. The `applicationDidBecomeActive` method will be called after this method, as the application is going from an inactive to active state.

`applicationWill ResignActive`	Notifies the delegate that the application is about to become inactive. This occurs when the application becomes interrupted, the user enables screen lock, or the user quits the application. An application interruption can be caused by an incoming phone call, SMS message, or alarm.
`applicationWill Terminate`	Notifies the application delegate that the app is about to terminate. This gets called for devices that do not support background execution or the device is running iOS 3.x or earlier.

In order to illustrate the application going through the different application states you should add **NSLog** messages to each of the delegate methods. You must modify the implementation file (*GameAppDelegate.m*) to appear as follows:

```
- (BOOL)application:(UIApplication *)application
  didFinishLaunchingWithOptions:(NSDictionary *)launchOptions
{
    self.window =
        [[UIWindow alloc]
        initWithFrame:[[UIScreen mainScreen] bounds]];

    NSLog(@"didFinishLaunchingWithOptions");

    self.viewController =
        [[GameViewController alloc]
        initWithNibName:@"GameViewController" bundle:nil];
    self.window.rootViewController = self.viewController;
    [self.window makeKeyAndVisible];
    return YES;
}

- (void)applicationWillResignActive:(UIApplication *)application
{
    NSLog(@"applicationWillResignActive");
}
```

```
- (void)applicationDidEnterBackground:
    (UIApplication *)application
{

    NSLog(@"applicationDidEnterBackground");
}

- (void)applicationWillEnterForeground:
    (UIApplication *)application
{

    NSLog(@"applicationWillEnterForeground");
}

- (void)applicationDidBecomeActive:(UIApplication *)application
{

    NSLog(@"applicationDidBecomeActive");
}

- (void)applicationWillTerminate:(UIApplication *)application
{

    NSLog(@"applicationWillTerminate");
}
```

Next, open the *GameViewController.m* implementation file that is the primary view controller for managing the view in this game. The view controller is notified when certain events happen to the view it is managing. This includes when the view is loaded or unloaded and when the view will appear or disappear. Modify the implementation so the code looks as follows:

```
- (void)viewDidLoad
{

    NSLog(@"viewDidLoad");
    [super viewDidLoad];
}
- (void)viewWillAppear:(BOOL)animated
{

    NSLog(@"viewWillAppear");
    [super viewWillAppear:animated];
}
```

```
- (void)viewDidAppear:(BOOL)animated
{
    NSLog(@"viewDidAppear");
    [super viewDidAppear:animated];
}
- (void)viewWillDisappear:(BOOL)animated
{
    NSLog(@"viewWillDisappear");
    [super viewWillDisappear:animated];
}
- (void)viewDidDisappear:(BOOL)animated
{
    NSLog(@"viewDidDisappear");
    [super viewDidDisappear:animated];
}
- (void)viewDidUnload
{
    NSLog(@"viewDidUnload");
    [super viewDidUnload];
}
```

Make sure the current scheme is set to run in the iOS Simulator and run the application. Once the application is displayed in the Simulator, look at the output in the Debug window, which shows log messages and the order that each method was called. It should look similar to the following:

```
2011-04-11 13:02:42.873 Game[22357:207] main
2011-04-11 13:02:43.207 Game[22357:207]
        didFinishLaunchingWithOptions
2011-04-11 13:02:43.208 Game[22357:207] viewDidLoad
2011-04-11 13:02:43.209 Game[22357:207] viewWillAppear
2011-04-11 13:02:43.210 Game[22357:207]
        applicationDidBecomeActive
2011-04-11 13:02:43.209 Game[22357:207] viewDidAppear
```

Note that after the main function is called, the first application delegate notification is didFinishLaunchingWithOptions. After that, you will receive notifications in the view controller that the view did load (viewDidLoad), will appear (viewWillAppear), and finally did appear (viewDidAppear). The application delegate is notified that the application became active (applicationDid BecomeActive) before the view finally appears.

Now quit the application by pressing the home button on the Simulator. The following messages are logged:

```
2011-04-11 13:07:00.238 Game[22357:207]
    applicationWillResignActive
2011-04-11 13:07:00.240 Game[22357:207]
    applicationDidEnterBackground
```

Now relaunch the application from the SpringBoard (home screen) by tapping on the application icon. The following messages appear in the log:

```
2011-04-11 13:07:01.563 Game[22357:207]
    applicationWillEnterForeground
2011-04-11 13:07:01.565 Game[22357:207]
    applicationDidBecomeActive
```

You have just walked through all the different application states that the game will go into. You should take note that the application was never shut down and applicationWillTerminate was not called. This will become important later in the development of the game, as you will need to at least handle pausing and resuming the game (especially when an animation timer is used). But I don't want to jump ahead of myself, as you need to first learn about Interface Builder and how it can be used to build the game interface.

Interface Builder

The first game you will create (Figure 1-12) will pose a math problem and allow the user to enter and submit an answer. If the answer is wrong it will let the user try again, and if it is correct then a new math problem will be generated.

Figure 1-12. Simple math game

You will use Interface Builder to design the interface and lay out all the controls that you will need. Single click on the *GameViewController.xib* file in the Project Navigator to display the nib file in Interface Builder, as shown in Figure 1-13. At this time, make sure you have the Utility view open (if it's not, click View→Utilities→Show Utilities), so you can use the various inspectors required to create interfaces.

You will notice next to the File Inspector and Quick Help that there are new inspectors to use in Interface Builder: Identity, Attributes, Size, and Connection Inspectors. At the bottom of the Utility Area you will find the library pane, which lists various things that can be added to a project. Make sure you've selected the Object Library (View→Utilities→Object Library) and you'll see UI controls that you can add to the view.

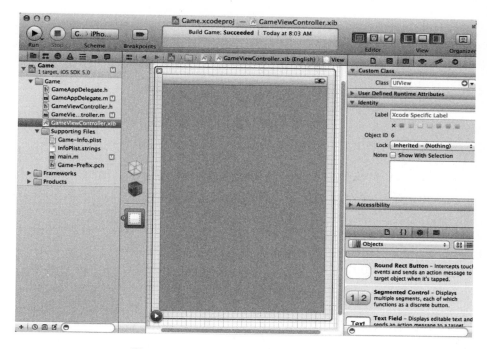

Figure 1-13. Interface Builder

The interface will use a label to ask a question, a text control to receive an answer, and a button to submit and check if the answer was correct. Drag a Label from the Object Library into the top center of the view in the main editor. Drag a Text Field under that and to the left. Drag out a Rounded Rect button to the right of the Text Field. When a Text Field is used for input, a keyboard appears that covers the bottom half of the iPhone screen. Because of this, you need to keep all of these controls located in the top half on the view. Figure 1-14 shows how to add these objects to the view.

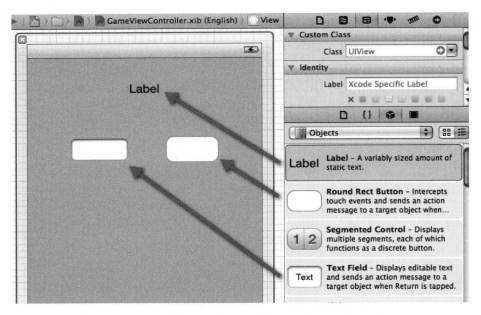

Figure 1-14. Dragging objects into the view

Switch to the Attributes Inspector and click on the Label. Change the Text to "Ask Question Here" and then adjust the size of the control so that it spans most of the view width. Change the text alignment to center. The label should now appear centered in the middle of the screen. If needed, you can drag the label around on the screen until you see a blue line appear in the center, which tells you the label is now located in the center of the containing view. Click on the Font button and modify the size to be 24. You may need to adjust the width and height of the control if you find the text getting clipped. I ended up sizing the control to be 280×40. You can also open the Size Inspector if you want specify the exact width and height of the control.

Now click on the Text Field and change the Placeholder text to **Answer**. The placeholder text displays when text has not been entered into the control and serves as a way to let the user know what type of input should be specified. You can also specify the type of keyboard that gets displayed when the user taps the control. Since the game is asking a math question, it makes since to display only numbers. Scroll down to the Keyboard attribute and change the value to **Number Pad**. In order to make the answer a little easier to read, let's adjust the font size to 18.

Click on the button and change the Title to display **Submit** inside of the button. You can also double-click on the button to modify the title in place. Adjust the height of the button to match the size of the text control. The interface should now appear similar to Figure 1-15.

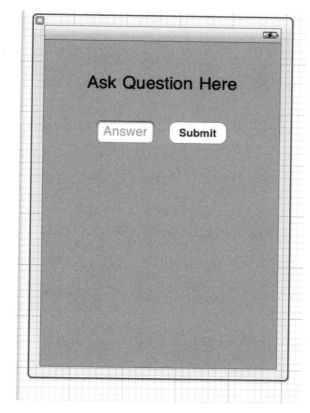

Figure 1-15. Interface Builder controls

Now that the interface has been created, you need to hook up the controls as properties of the view controller. This will allow you to change the label text, read the answer, and add logic to handle the tapping of the Submit button.

Connections

It is time to bridge the gap between the interface and the code. You do this by creating referencing outlets between the controls contained in the view and the view controller. The easiest way to do this in Xcode is to use the secondary assistant so that both the interface and the header file of the view controller are displayed next to each other. You may need to enable the secondary editor on the Editor segment control located on the toolbar, as shown in Figure 1-16, or by selecting View→Editor→Assistant from the menu.

Figure 1-16. Showing the secondary editor using the toolbar

The secondary editor will display the appropriate file in the secondary area, in this case it will be the *GameViewController.h* file. If you do not see this file in the secondary editor, you may need to change the editor to **Automatic** in the jump bar, as shown in Figure 1-17.

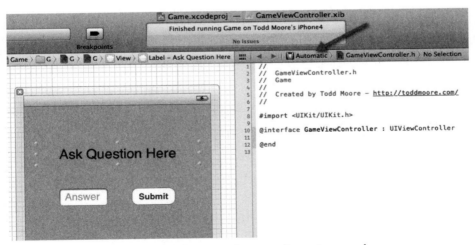

Figure 1-17. Secondary editor jump bar

Control-click on the top label to display the label properties for the control. Create a new referencing outlet by clicking in the circle to the right of New Referencing Outlet and dragging to just below the **GameViewController** interface definition. As you are dragging you will see a line being drawn, as shown in Figure 1-18, and also the location of where the outlet will be inserted.

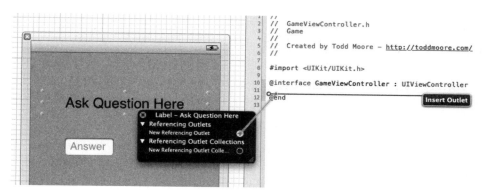

Figure 1-18. Creating a New Referencing Outlet

Make sure you release the mouse button when you see the "Insert Outlet" marker displayed before the **@end** statement. You will now receive a pop-up that allows you to specify the name of the property, as shown in Figure 1-19. Type "label" in as the Name of the property and click Connect.

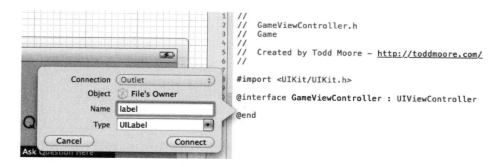

Figure 1-19. Creating a new connection

You will repeat this operation again for the answer text field, but this time will use a shortcut to make the connection. Control-drag directly from the text field (without releasing the mouse button) and draw a line to the interface file right below the previous property definition. Once the insert marker is in the appropriate position, release the drag operation, and when prompted type in "answer" as the Name of this property. If you have done this correctly, the interface file should appear as follows:

```
@interface GameViewController : UIViewController

@property (retain, nonatomic) IBOutlet UILabel *label;
@property (retain, nonatomic) IBOutlet UITextField *answer;

@end
```

Now repeat the same operation for the button, but instead of creating a property you will create an action. When the connection pop-up appears, change the connection type from Outlet to Action. Now type in "submit" as the Name of the new method. You should see the following added to the interface file:

```
- (IBAction)submit:(id)sender;
```

You have successfully connected the label and text field as properties and added a submit method that will be called when the button is tapped. Xcode has not only been editing the interface file for us, but also adding code into the implementation file. Let's open up the *GameViewController.m* file and look at what was added:

```
- (void)viewDidUnload
{
    NSLog(@"viewDidUnload");
    [self setLabel:nil];
    [self setAnswer:nil];
    [super viewDidUnload];
    // Release any retained subviews of the main view.
    // e.g. self.myOutlet = nil;
}
```

The `viewDidUnload` method now sets the label and answer properties to nil. Xcode makes sure the program won't have a memory leak by setting the properties to `nil` in the `viewDidUnload` method, which causes the controls to be released.

The default behavior for low memory conditions is to release views that do not have a superview. This could be views on the screen that are not currently displayed or active. It is extremely important whenever controls are connected as retained properties of the view controller that they are properly released in both the `dealloc` and `viewDidUnload` methods. I've seen a lot of strange issues occur in apps that were caused by incorrect handling of `viewDidUnload`. Always make sure retained user interface properties are set to `nil` so they will be released and memory freed. Also, if you programmatically added views in the `viewDidLoad` function, then you usually will need to remove those views in `viewDidUnload` so the view can be properly unloaded. The view controller will reload the view again when it is needed and all properties will be reconnected. Always test low memory conditions in the Simulator by selecting Simulate Memory Warning from the Hardware menu.

As you previously discovered, apps running on iOS 4 do not shut down but instead go into a suspended state. An application that never terminates means you really need to make sure you are allocating and deallocating objects correctly. An application with a memory leak may at some point consume so much memory that it will be killed by the system. This would leave a bad impression on your users, as they would think your application has bugs (which it does!). Interface Builder helps to make the process easier by adding code to release the properties in the `dealloc` and `viewDidUnload` functions.

You will also notice a submit method has been stubbed out for us to implement. This method was connected as an action and will be called when the user taps the button:

```
- (IBAction)submit:(id)sender
{
}
```

Now that you have created the interface and made all the connections it is finally time to do some coding.

Game Logic

You will write code to ask a math problem and then wait for the user to submit an answer. Once submitted it will alert the user if the provided answer was correct or not. If the answer was correct then a new question is generated. If the answer was wrong then it will allow the user to try again.

You will first create a method that generates a math problem and records the correct answer. Add the following to the *GameViewController.m* implementation file above the #pragma directive that appears before **viewDidLoad** function:

```
- (void)generate
{
    // pick two numbers between 1 and 9
    int a = 1 + arc4random() % 9;
    int b = 1 + arc4random() % 9;

    // calculate the sum
    int sum = a + b;

    // create our question
    label.text = [NSString
    stringWithFormat:
      @"%d + %d = ", a, b];

    // save the answer in the tag property of the label
    label.tag = sum;
}
```

This function picks two numbers between 1 and 9 using the **arc4random()** function. The **arc4random()** function is the preferred way of generating random numbers. It does not require seeding like the **rand()** or **random()** functions you may have used if you've done any C programming. The sum is then calculated and the text of the label is updated to ask what "a + b =" by creating an **NSString** and using the **stringWithFormat** method. This method is very similar to **printf** (used in C programming) in that variable arguments can be specified in the creation of a string. I am utilizing the tag property of the label to store the answer. The **tag** variable is available in all **UIView** derived classes and is mainly used for identification purposes, but you can set it to any integer value because it is there for your use only and has no bearing on the control or its behavior.

Now you need to call the generate function when the view loads. This will make sure the label has a question already loaded before the view actually displays. Modify the **viewDidLoad** implementation to appear as follows (the line you must add is shown in bold):

```
- (void)viewDidLoad
{
    NSLog(@"viewDidLoad");
    [super viewDidLoad];

    [self generate];
}
```

In the submit method you will check if the answer given is the correct one and generate an alert message to the user. Modify the **submit** function to appear as follows:

```
- (IBAction)submit:(id)sender
{
    // convert our answer text value into an integer
    int num = [answer.text intValue];

    // check if it is correct by comparing to the label tag
    UIAlertView *alert;
    if (num == label.tag)
    {
        // answer was correct
```

```
        alert = [[UIAlertView alloc]
                    initWithTitle:@"Correct"
                    message:@"Let's try another one!"
                    delegate:self
                    cancelButtonTitle:@"OK"
                    otherButtonTitles: nil];

        // use the alert tag to mark that answer was correct
        alert.tag = 1;
    } else
    {
        // answer is incorrect
        alert = [[UIAlertView alloc]
                    initWithTitle:@"Wrong!"
                    message:@"That answer is incorrect."
                    delegate:self
                    cancelButtonTitle:@"Try Again"
                    otherButtonTitles: nil];
    }

    // show and release the alert
    [alert show];
    [alert release];
}
```

The submit function first retrieves the answer from the text field as an integer value. Since the **text** property is an **NSString**, you can use the **intValue** method to convert the string value into an integer. Now that you have the answer as an integer, you can compare it to the **tag** property that was set in the label to see if the answer was correct. You then create an alert message with either a correct or incorrect message. I am utilizing the **tag** property of the **UIAlertView** to store if the answer was correct or not. The **tag** is by default set to 0, so you will set it to 1 when the answer is correct.

You will now need to handle when the user dismisses the alert view and check the **tag** variable to see if the answer was correct. If it was correct then you will generate a new question and clear out the previous answer. Insert this code below the submit method:

```objc
- (void)alertView:(UIAlertView *)alertView
          clickedButtonAtIndex:(NSInteger)buttonIndex
{
    if (alertView.tag == 1)
    {
        // generate a new question
        [self generate];

        // reset our previous answer
        answer.text = @"";
    }
}
```

Now build and run the game either in the Simulator or on the device. Tap the answer control to bring up the keyboard, which will allow you to specify numeric value. Try providing both correct and wrong answers to verify the game logic.

As a final touch, I want to have the keyboard display automatically when the application launches. This way the user can just specify the answer immediately instead of having to tap the control first to display the keyboard. In order to do this, you need to specify that the answer control is the first responder. This has the same effect as tapping on the control, so the keyboard will appear as soon as the view is displayed. Modify the existing **viewDidAppear** method to the following:

```objc
- (void)viewDidAppear:(BOOL)animated
{
    NSLog(@"viewDidAppear");
    [super viewDidAppear:animated];
    [self.answer becomeFirstResponder];
}
```

And there you have it, you just created a simple math game using only a few lines of code. In the next chapter, you will create a more sophisticated game that uses animation, collision detection, and multi-touch.

2
Hello Pong

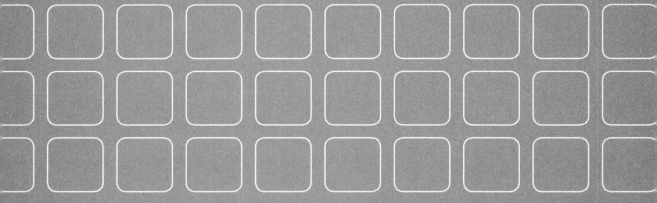

My addiction to playing video games started when my father purchased Atari's Home Pong console. It plugged into a standard television, had two controllers, and displayed only in black and white. There were two white rectangles on each side of the screen that represented each player's paddle. The controller had a rotating dial that placed the paddles into different vertical positions. There was a puck that was represented by a small white square that bounced off the walls and player paddles. Each successful paddle hit would increase the puck speed which in turn made it more difficult to hit. If a player missed the puck then a point would be awarded to the other player and the round would reset, putting the puck speed back to normal.

Although Pong didn't sport flashy graphics and sounds, it had all the typical elements that current games have: an objective to accomplish, player representation in a world, a score that measures progress, and a way to finish the game. The Atari engineer that designed and built Pong was given the project as a training exercise to help him get acclimated at creating games. I feel that this exercise holds up even today as a great way to teach how to create a game on the iPhone (see Figure 2-1). You will learn how to implement multi-touch controls, animation, collision detection, and scoring.

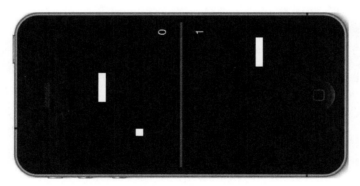

Figure 2-1. The Paddles game running in the iPhone Simulator

Project Creation

You need to start by opening Xcode and creating a new project (File→New→New Project) from scratch called Paddles. Select the iOS/Application/Single View Application template, and click Next. Enter "Paddles" as the product name and Class Prefix, put in your company identifier, change the Device Family to iPhone, and deselect the three checkboxes below. Click Next, as shown in Figure 2-2. Choose a location for this new project and click Create.

Once Xcode generates the new project, Xcode opens the target settings page, where you will need to adjust a few settings. You'll see how to do that next.

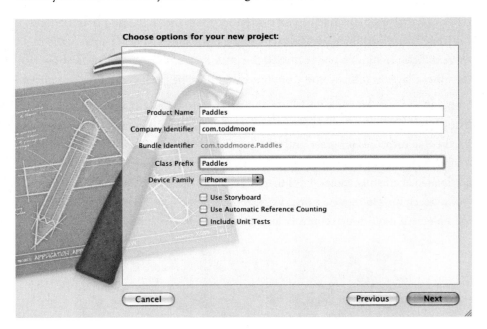

Figure 2-2. Creating a new project: Paddles

Target Settings

The Summary page for the Paddles Target displays a few items of importance, including the supported devices and the Deployment Target version. The Devices pop-up lets you choose to support either iPhone, iPad, or Universal (which supports both devices in a single application). Leave supported devices set to iPhone and change the Deployment Target to 3.0, which will allow the application to install on iOS versions 3.0 and greater, as shown in Figure 2-3. It is always best to keep the version number as low as possible, as you don't want to exclude customers that may be slow to upgrade their device. The game you are creating does not require features found only in newer versions of iOS.

> Apps that use features that require a version greater than your deployment target will crash devices running earlier iOS versions. It is important to handle version checks at runtime or raise your minimum deployment target to match the features you are using. Always check the iOS documentation for the minimum iOS version required.

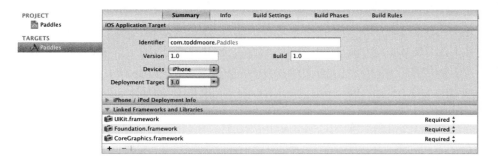

Figure 2-3. Target settings and configuring Deployment Target to 3.0

You can also specify what the Supported Device Orientations will be for your application—Portrait, Portrait Upside Down, Landscape Left, and Landscape Right. This is more important for iPad apps because they can launch into any orientation (and must display different splash screens depending on orientation). However, this could change for iPhone apps in the future, so it is best practice to tell iOS which orientations the application supports. The Paddles game will only support portrait mode orientation, so make sure that the Portrait button is the only item selected.

Next, you'll need to make some changes to the App Info file.

> The view controller class also specifies orientations that the underlying views will support. The default implementation is to only support Portrait mode, but the generated project code might override this to support additional orientations. Open the *PaddlesViewController.h* file and remove the `shouldAutorotateToInterfaceOrientation` method if it exists. This will ensure the view controller will not rotate our view while playing the game.

App Info

iPhone games will typically want to use the entire real estate of the screen, which means hiding the status bar. The App Info file contains many settings that describe the application to iOS, including the app version, icon files, and the display name. This information can be edited by either expanding the *Supporting Files* folder and opening *Paddles-Info.plist* or by selecting the Info tab from the Paddles Target. There are many settings that are not visible by default and hiding the status bar is one of them. You can add a new item by clicking on an existing row and clicking the plus icon or by option clicking to the pop-up menu and choosing Add Row. Use the dropdown to the right of the Key name entry to change it to "Status bar is initially hidden" and set its value to YES, as shown in Figure 2-4. The reason you want to do this here and not within code is that with this setting, the system will slowly fade the status bar out when the application is loading. It looks much better to have iOS animate the status bar away while the app loads rather than waiting for the app to load and then hiding it.

Key	Type	Value
Localization native development region	String	en
Bundle display name	String	${PRODUCT_NAME}
Executable file	String	${EXECUTABLE_NAME}
▶ Icon files	Array	(0 items)
Bundle identifier	String	com.toddmoore.${PRODUCT_NAME:rfc1034identifier}
InfoDictionary version	String	6.0
Bundle name	String	${PRODUCT_NAME}
Bundle OS Type code	String	APPL
Bundle versions string, short	String	1.0
Bundle creator OS Type code	String	????
Bundle version	String	1.0
Application requires iPhone environmer	Boolean	YES
▶ Required device capabilities	Array	(1 item)
▶ Supported interface orientations	Array	(1 item)
Status bar is initially hidden ⬍ ⊕ ⊖	Boolean	YES ⬍

Figure 2-4. Removing status bar from the iOS application

Laying Out the Game Pieces

I created my first iPhone game without using Interface Builder. This meant that I had to allocate all my views, images, and labels by hand and tweak their position and size until it looked right. Everything that I could quickly do in Interface Builder, I wrote out in source code, which was extremely tedious and error prone. If I could go back in time and give myself a 30 minute lesson on how to use Interface Builder's powerful WYSIWYG (what you see is what you get) editor then my game would have been finished much sooner.

Interface Builder

In the Project Navigator, click on the *PaddlesViewController.xib* file that displays Interface Builder in the Xcode Editor Area and allows you to modify the user interface. Next, make sure the Utilities view's Attributes Inspector is open (click View→Utilities→Attributes Inspector). The Utilities view appears on the right side of Xcode and lets you choose from several inspectors by using the toolbar at its top. In Figure 2-5, the Attributes Inspector is shown at the top with the Object Library at the bottom. Click on the lone view that is sitting in the center of the Interface Builder window. Next, you'll see how to use the Attributes Inspector to modify various properties for this, the *root view*.

Now is a good time to familiarize yourself with the other inspectors available in the Utilities view. Hover your mouse pointer over the inspector icons to reveal the name of each inspector.

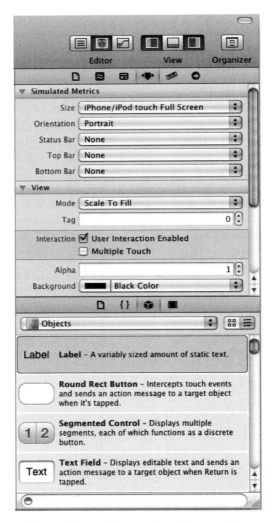

Figure 2-5. Utility Area, Attributes Inspector,
and Object Library

Change the View background color from Grey to Black. Change the Status Bar under Simulated Metrics to None since it will not be displayed in the game. The status bar reserves 20 pixels in height from the total screen height of 480 pixels. This means the root view is 460 pixels in height when the status bar is displayed. Click the Size Inspector tool, shown in Figure 2-6, and make sure the height is set to 480, which matches the screen height dimension without the status bar.

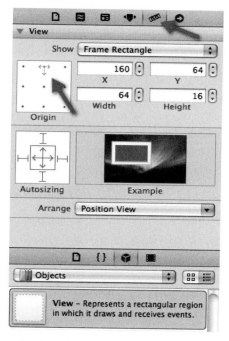

Figure 2-6. Size Inspector and setting origin

The Object Library view is located at the bottom of the Utility Area under the inspectors and allows you to drag new UI controls into the view. There are many objects to choose from, such as buttons, labels, and images. I will start with the most basic of elements, which is the View and the object that all user interface elements inherit from. The View object has properties such as frame dimensions and a background color. This is really all that is needed at the moment because the paddles and puck will be represented by white rectangles.

Scroll down the list of elements until you find View and drag it onto the existing root view so that it becomes a subview or child of the existing root view. Adjust the size of this view to be 64 pixels in width and 16 pixels in height, which represents one of the paddles. You need to position this paddle at the top but leave enough room for your finger to sit behind the paddle.

Click the Origin pane and change focus to center top, shown with the leftmost arrow in Figure 2-6, which will adjust the origin numbers to match that location on the paddle relative to the containing view. Adjust the X position of the paddle to be centered at 160 pixels from the left of the screen. Adjust the Y position to be 64 pixels down from the top of the screen.

Copy and paste this paddle to create the second paddle of the same size. You want the second paddle to be the same distance from the bottom of the screen as the first paddle was from the top. The total height of the view is 480 so you need to take the first visible pixel, which would be at 479, and subtract 64 from it (479 – 64 = 415). Change the origin pane to set focus on the center bottom of the new paddle and adjust the position to 160, 415. Both paddles should now be centered and be the same distance from their edge of the screen.

Create the puck by dragging another view in and resizing it to 16×16. Now click on the Arrange Position View drop-down and click Center Horizontally In The Container. Click Arrange Position View again and then Center Vertically In The Container. The puck should now be located directly in the center of the view.

I want to add a middle line down the center of the screen that will help visualize each player's side of the screen. Drag another view in and size it to 320×5. Center it vertically and horizontally like you just did with the puck. Click to the Attributes Inspector and change the Background color to Grey. Notice the line is placed on top of the puck because it was the last view added.

You can change the order of the view objects by using the Outline View located immediately to the left of the editor. You may need to expand it by clicking the Outline view button in the dock. This pane displays a hierarchical tree that reflects the parent-child relationships between the objects in the nib file. The view objects at the bottom of the list are drawn on top of those higher in the list. Drag the middle line up to be the first entry in the Objects view hierarchy, as shown in Figure 2-7. The middle line will now be drawn under the puck object. You could have also selected Editor→Arrangement→Send to Back from the menu to perform the same operation.

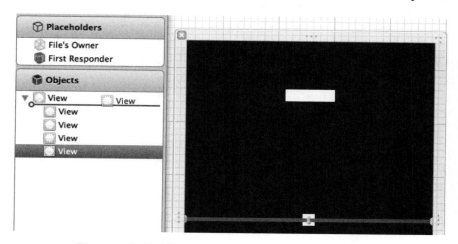

Figure 2-7. Changing the view hierarchy

Connections

As in the previous chapter, you will need to enable the secondary editor so the associated **PaddlesViewController** header file is displayed next to the Interface Builder editor. Control-drag from the top paddle to just below the **UIViewController** interface definition. As you are dragging, you will see a line being drawn, as shown in Figure 2-8, as well as the location of where the outlet will be inserted.

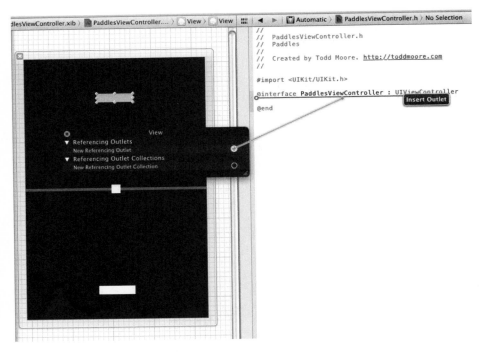

Figure 2-8. Connect outlets directly to source code to automatically insert properties

As soon as you release the mouse button, you will receive a pop-up that lets you specify the connection type, name of the object, and object type. The connection should stay as an Outlet, set the name to **viewPaddle1**, and keep the type set to **UIView**. Repeat this process for the other paddle and the puck, which will leave the interface looking as follows:

```
@interface PaddlesViewController : UIViewController

@property (nonatomic, retain) IBOutlet UIView *viewPaddle1;
@property (nonatomic, retain) IBOutlet UIView *viewPaddle2;
@property (nonatomic, retain) IBOutlet UIView *viewPuck;

@end
```

Open the *PaddlesViewController.m* implementation file and you will notice, as in the previous chapter, the views are being released in the **dealloc** and **viewDid Unload** functions:

```
- (void)dealloc
{
    [viewPaddle1 release];
    [viewPaddle2 release];
    [viewPuck release];
    [super dealloc];
}

- (void)viewDidUnload
{
    [self setViewPaddle1:nil];
    [self setViewPaddle2:nil];
    [self setViewPuck:nil];
    [super viewDidUnload];
}
```

Now that you have connected the two paddles and puck as properties of the controller, you have access to their position on the screen and can manipulate them as needed. The next step will be to control the paddles using multi-touch.

Multi-touch

Apple's introduction of the original iPhone brought the world an impressive list of innovations in a really small device. Multi-touch is certainly at the top of that list, and even though touch screens have been around for a long time, it was Apple that showed the world how the technology could be effectively used in a consumer product. They built the whole user interface of the operating system around the concept of touch and multi-touch. The interfaces they designed were intuitive and easy to use, which ultimately led to the iPhone becoming extremely popular. Traditional desktop operating systems have attempted to add touch, but it typically has been implemented by just mapping your touch position to the current mouse position. That just doesn't have the same feel as an iOS device, which was designed from the ground up to have touch be its primary form of input.

You may find touch to be initially similar to handling mouse events, but there are plenty of differences. The first and most obvious is there can be multiple positions on the screen at the same time. The original iPhone supports tracking up to five touch locations at the same time. The second difference, which may not seem so obvious, is that touch doesn't always have a position on the screen. If you are not touching the screen then there is no position at all. Compare that to a mouse which always has a position on the screen represented by a pointer. Even if you do not move the mouse, it still has an active position on the screen and as a developer you can query the system to retrieve that position. Because of these reasons, I will cover how touch events work in more detail and the best practices for tracking multiple touches on the screen.

Four Methods of Touch

Multi-touch is handled by adding four methods to your view controller object. The system will call these methods whenever a touch changes into a different state. The **touchesBegan** method is called when a touch is first detected on the screen. The **touchesMoved** method will follow if the touch moves into a new position. And finally, **touchesEnded** will be called when the touch is lifted off the screen. It is possible that the **touchesEnded** method may not be called if the system decides to cancel the touch. In this case, the **touchesCancelled** will be called in its place. This can occur when the application gets interrupted by another function, such as the device receiving a text message or phone call.

Let's implement code into the view controller that will log each touch method to the Debug window. Insert this code into the *PaddlesViewController.m* implementation file:

```
- (void)touchesBegan:(NSSet *)touches withEvent:(UIEvent *)event
{
    NSLog(@"touchesBegan");
}
- (void)touchesMoved:(NSSet *)touches withEvent:(UIEvent *)event
{
    NSLog(@"touchesMoved");
}
- (void)touchesEnded:(NSSet *)touches withEvent:(UIEvent *)event
```

```
{
    NSLog(@"touchesEnded");
}
- (void)touchesCancelled:(NSSet *)touches
               withEvent:(UIEvent *)event
{
    NSLog(@"touchesCancelled");
}
```

Make sure Xcode is displaying the Debug window by enabling it from the toolbar or selecting View→Show Debug Area from the menu. Run the program in the Simulator and click the Simulator screen very quickly. The output window should display something similar to the following:

```
2011-03-23 12:03:28.791 Paddles[6007:207] touchesBegan
2011-03-23 12:03:28.990 Paddles[6007:207] touchesEnded
```

Notice that it is possible that move events may not be generated during a touch sequence, however, there is always a **touchesBegan** event followed by either a **touchesEnded** or **touchesCancelled** event. Now click and drag your mouse across the Simulator screen. You will notice this results in multiple move events occurring between the **touches Began** and **touchesEnded** events.

```
2011-03-23 12:04:09.025 Paddles[6007:207] touchesBegan
2011-03-23 12:04:10.884 Paddles[6007:207] touchesMoved
2011-03-23 12:04:10.933 Paddles[6007:207] touchesMoved
2011-03-23 12:04:11.066 Paddles[6007:207] touchesMoved
2011-03-23 12:04:11.766 Paddles[6007:207] touchesEnded
```

Enable Multi-touch

At this point you have been using the Simulator to monitor each of the touch events. The Simulator can emulate two touches by holding down the Option key while clicking but it is very limited and best suited for pinch zooming. This is why it is best to test on an actual device when coding multi-touch. Connect an iOS device and then change the active project scheme to target the connected device.

If you build and run the application on the device and put two fingers on the screen you will notice the second touch is being ignored. This is because views, by default, ignore multiple touches. You have to specifically enable multi-touch for any view that requires it. You could do this within code by modifying the `multipleTouchEnabled` property of the root view or use Interface Builder to enable Multiple Touch, as shown in Figure 2-9.

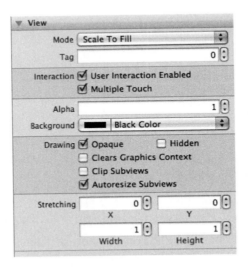

Figure 2-9. Enable Multi-Touch using
Interface Builder

The touch methods in the view controller will now be called for all touches on the screen. It is important to know that each **UITouch** object is guaranteed to be the same instantiation throughout the entire touch life cycle from start to finish. This means that the each individual touch on the screen is represented by the same **UITouch** object throughout all of the callbacks. In order to see this, add the following code snippet into all of the touch methods that you just added:

```
for (UITouch *touch in touches)
{
    NSLog(@" - %p", touch);
}
```

This code will print out the memory address location of every **UITouch** object contained in the set. If you run this on device and place two fingers on the screen you will see output similar to the following:

```
2011-03-23 14:48:05.015 Paddles[2962:307] touchesBegan
2011-03-23 14:48:05.019 Paddles[2962:307]  - 0x12eed0
2011-03-23 14:48:05.021 Paddles[2962:307]  - 0x12f3b0
2011-03-23 14:48:05.077 Paddles[2962:307] touchesMoved
2011-03-23 14:48:05.080 Paddles[2962:307]  - 0x12eed0
2011-03-23 14:48:05.083 Paddles[2962:307] touchesEnded
2011-03-23 14:48:05.086 Paddles[2962:307]  - 0x12f3b0
2011-03-23 14:48:05.093 Paddles[2962:307] touchesEnded
2011-03-23 14:48:05.096 Paddles[2962:307]  - 0x12eed0
```

Notice in the above example that two touches came into **touchesBegan** at the same time at address locations **0x12eed0** and **0x12f3b0**. The touch at address **0x12eed0** then moves while the other touch does not. I know the other touch did not move because it was not included as part of the set. The touch at **0x12f3b0** then goes into an Ended state followed by the **0x12eed0** touch. At this point, both touches have finished and the address locations could be reused by the system. This is just a simple example of two touches on the screen at the same time. In your testing, you will probably notice a lot more log messages being generated and multiple touches being passed in through all the different touch methods.

Moving Paddles

You will now modify the touch handlers to move each paddle horizontally along the x-axis. In order to get the actual touch position within the view, you need to call upon a method of the **UITouch** object called **locationInView**. This method will return the position of the touch relative to the view provided. You will provide the root view, which has dimensions set to the full size of the screen. The return value is a **CGPoint**, which is a structure containing the X and Y position. The screen is 480 pixels in height, so you can use the Y value of this point to determine which paddle should be moved. If it is on the top half of the screen or less than 240 pixels, you move **paddle1**. If it is on the bottom half, you move **paddle2**. The paddle should only move along the x-axis so you need to set the new center position to be the X value of the touch point while keeping the Y value the same as it was before. You can make use of **CGPointMake**, which is a quick way to initialize a new **CGPoint** structure. Replace the previous implementation of **touchesBegan** with the following code:

```objc
- (void)touchesBegan:(NSSet *)touches withEvent:(UIEvent *)event
{
    // iterate through our touch elements
    for (UITouch *touch in touches)
    {
        // get the point of touch within the view
        CGPoint touchPoint = [touch locationInView: self.view];

        // move the paddle based on which half of screen the
        // touch falls into
        if (touchPoint.y < 240)
        {
            viewPaddle1.center = CGPointMake(touchPoint.x,
                                        viewPaddle1.center.y);
        }
        else
        {
            viewPaddle2.center = CGPointMake(touchPoint.x,
                                        viewPaddle2.center.y);
        }
    }
}
```

The code above handles initial touches but does not handle if those touches move along the screen. The paddles will be controlled by leaving your finger on the screen and moving it back and forth, so you also need to handle the **touches Moved** event. You can just call the **touchesBegan** handler for now to reuse the paddle-moving logic. Replace the previous implementation of **touchesMoved** with the following code:

```objc
- (void)touchesMoved:(NSSet *)touches withEvent:(UIEvent *)event
{
    [self touchesBegan: touches withEvent: event];
}
```

Run this code on the device and notice that you can move both paddles at the same time using multiple touches. Not bad for just a few lines of code! Keep playing with the paddles and see if you can find any issues with the current implementation. There are two problems that I want to address in the next section.

Multi-touch Issues: Third Finger on the Glassy Knoll

The person that will be controlling the paddle will typically start by placing their finger behind their own paddle on their side of the screen. They will move their finger back and forth and usually not let up until the game has finished. There are two issues with the current implementation that you may have noticed. The first is you can slide your touch across the middle line and it will move the other player's paddle. As shown in Figure 2-10, player two moves their finger up past the middle line and to the left. This would result in player one's paddle moving out of the path of the puck resulting in an unfair point given to player two. The second issue is if there are any additional touches on the screen they will also affect the player's paddle position. The third finger on the screen, also shown in Figure 2-10, would cause player one's paddle to jump out of the path of the puck resulting again in an unfair point given to player two. Both of these conditions should be prevented so the game will not suffer from years of conspiracy theories about what really happened that day you played air hockey on the glassy knoll.

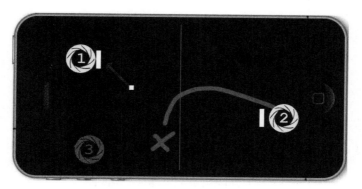

Figure 2-10. Issues with current implementation

This game should be no different from a real game of table tennis in terms of paddle control. In a real game of table tennis, once someone grabs a paddle, that paddle stays with them at all times until they are finished playing. In this game, the expected behavior should be the same. Once a player has control over a paddle then that paddle cannot be controlled by another until they let go of it. Therefore, you should ignore any additional touches that occur on that players side. In addition, if a player already has an assigned paddle then they should not be able to control another paddle such as when crossing the middle line. In order to solve this you need to track which touch belongs to which paddle. As previously discussed, touch objects will always be the same object instantiation throughout the entire life cycle of touch events. You can use that fact in order to bind a specific touch to a specific paddle.

Touch the Right Way

In order to track specific touch objects to each paddle, you will add a couple variables into the **PaddlesViewController** interface. You will use **touch1** as the active touch bound to **paddle1** and **touch2** as the active touch bound to **paddle2**. If a paddle is not assigned a touch then it will be assigned a **nil** value. Add the following variables into the *PaddlesViewController.h* interface definition so it appears as follows:

```
@interface PaddlesViewController : UIViewController
{
    UITouch *touch1;
    UITouch *touch2;
}
```

You will modify the **touchesBegan** implementation to assign the paddle to a specific touch only if it is unassigned. You still want to use the logic that requires the touch to be placed at the top half of the screen to be assigned to **paddle1** and bottom half of screen for **paddle2**. If those conditions are met then you will assign the correct touch object to the paddle and move the paddle to the position of the touch as coded previously. Replace the previous implementation of **touchesBegan** with the following code:

```
- (void)touchesBegan:(NSSet *)touches withEvent:(UIEvent *)event
{
    // iterate through our touch elements
    for (UITouch *touch in touches)
```

```
{
    // get the point of touch within the view
    CGPoint touchPoint = [touch locationInView: self.view];

    // check which half of the screen touch is on and assign
    // it to a specific paddle if not already assigned
    if (touch1 == nil && touchPoint.y < 240)
    {
        touch1 = touch;
        viewPaddle1.center = CGPointMake(touchPoint.x,
                                viewPaddle1.center.y);
    }
    else if (touch2 == nil && touchPoint.y >= 240)
    {
        touch2 = touch;
        viewPaddle2.center = CGPointMake(touchPoint.x,
                                viewPaddle2.center.y);

    }
    }
}
```

Now that you have assigned specific touches to each paddle, you need to handle movement of the paddles. You can no longer just call the **touchesBegan** function because paddles that have already been assigned a specific touch will be ignored. Instead, you need to check if any of the touch objects provided in the set equals one of the touches that has been assigned to a paddle. If you receive an update to one of the assigned paddles then you can move it. It is safe to ignore all other touches that have not been assigned a paddle. Replace the previous implementation of **touchesMoved** with the following code:

```
- (void)touchesMoved:(NSSet *)touches withEvent:(UIEvent *)event
{
    // iterate through our touch elements
    for (UITouch *touch in touches)
    {
        // get the point of touch within the view
        CGPoint touchPoint = [touch locationInView: self.view];

        // if the touch is assigned to our paddle then move it
        if (touch == touch1)
```

```
    {
        viewPaddle1.center = CGPointMake(touchPoint.x,
                                         viewPaddle1.center.y);
    }
    else if (touch == touch2)
    {
        viewPaddle2.center = CGPointMake(touchPoint.x,
                                         viewPaddle2.center.y);
    }
  }
}
```

You need to handle when a paddle with an assigned touch has been lifted off the screen by implementing the **touchesEnded** handler. If any of the touches provided in the set equals one of the assigned touches of a paddle, then the assigned touch should be unbound from the paddle by setting the value to nil. If you didn't do this then you would most likely lose control of the paddle once the player lifted their finger off the screen. This would be the equivalent of the controller becoming unplugged from the console, which would not be good! Replace the previous implementation of **touchesEnded** with the following code:

```
- (void)touchesEnded:(NSSet *)touches withEvent:(UIEvent *)event
{
    // iterate through our touch elements
    for (UITouch *touch in touches)
    {
        if (touch == touch1) touch1 = nil;
            else if (touch == touch2) touch2 = nil;
    }
}
```

You need to also make sure to handle the cancelled event, and the same code written for the **touchesEnded** handler can be reused in this case. Remember that this method is called when the touch has been interrupted. You can test this event by either calling the device if it is an iPhone or by setting an alarm for iPod touch. Before the interruption is displayed, you will notice that all touches will be cancelled. If you did not handle the cancelled event, the players would most likely not be able to control their paddles after the interruption completed. Replace the previous implementation of **touchesCancelled** with the following code:

```
- (void)touchesCancelled:(NSSet *)touches
               withEvent:(UIEvent *)event
{
    [self touchesEnded:touches withEvent:event];
}
```

Run it on the device and notice once your initial touch has been assigned to a paddle, additional touches will not alter the position of that paddle. Also notice that if an assigned touch slides across the middle line that it will not affect the other paddle. The game now has a solid implementation of multi-touch.

Animation

You have the paddles moving based on where each player touches the screen, so now it's time to put the puck into motion. The game needs an animation loop that will move the puck in a specific direction and at a specific speed. Add the following variables to track direction and speed into the **PaddlesViewController** interface:

```
float dx;
float dy;
float speed;
```

The **dx** and **dy** variables represent the direction the puck is travelling and the speed represents how fast the puck is moving. I like to track speed and direction as separate variables so it is easier to speed up the puck while the game progresses. The **dx** variable is the direction the puck is travelling along the x-axis. If **dx** is −1 then the puck is moving left, if it is 0 then it is not moving, and if 1 then it is moving to the right. The **dy** variable represents the direction the puck is travelling along the y-axis. The **dy** variable will move the puck upwards if −1 and downwards if it is 1. The direction can also be any value between −1 and 1 so the puck can be moving on the screen at any angle.

You need a way to reset this information at the beginning of every round so you will add a function to handle initialization. The position and direction of the puck should be set to random values at the start of the game and the start of each round. You will again use the **arc4random()** function, as you did in the math game, but this time it will be used to pick either –1 or 1. Add the following **reset** function into the implementation file:

```
- (void)reset
{
    // set direction of ball to either left or right direction
    if ((arc4random() % 2) == 0) dx = -1; else dx = 1;

    // reverse dy if not 0 as this will send the puck to the
    // player who just scored otherwise set in random direction
    if (dy != 0) dy = -dy;
        else if ((arc4random() % 2) == 0) dy = -1; else dy = 1;

    // move point to random position in center
    viewPuck.center = CGPointMake(15 + arc4random() % (320-30),
                                  240);

    // reset speed
    speed = 2;
}
```

In the above code, I set the **dx** variable to randomly be either –1 or 1. This means the puck will either be moving left or right at the start of the round. I also set the **dy** variable to be either –1 or 1 if it is currently 0. However, if it is not 0 then it will reverse the direction. I did this because at the start of a game the puck should go toward a random paddle, but after a point is scored by a player I want it to go in the opposite direction so the player who scored the point has to hit the puck first.

The reset function also changes the position of the puck to be dropped somewhere along the center line. The speed is adjusted to 2, which is how many pixels the puck moves in a single frame of animation. Why did I select 2? I initially had it set to 1 but it just seemed too slow.

Add a simple animation function that moves the puck from its current center position into a new position offset by direction and speed. The animate function will be called repeatedly while the game is being played. Add the following code below the **reset** function:

```
- (void)animate
{
    // move puck to new position based on direction and speed
    viewPuck.center = CGPointMake(viewPuck.center.x + dx*speed,
                                  viewPuck.center.y + dy*speed);
}
```

Add an **NSTimer** to the **PaddlesViewController** interface:

```
NSTimer *timer;
```

You will schedule this timer to repeatedly call the animate function at an interval of 1/60, or 60 frames a second. The code also makes sure the puck is visible when the animation starts, and hides it when the animation has stopped. This has the effect of taking the puck off the field, which will be useful if the game is ever paused. That logic will be added later.

> The screen refresh rate for the iPhone is 60 Hz, which means the display gets refreshed 60 times a second. Performing animation logic faster than the screen refresh rate could cause some frames of animation to be skipped. For smooth animation it is best practice to schedule the timer as close to the screen refresh rate as possible.

Add the following code below the **reset** function, which will start and stop the game animation timer:

```
- (void)start
{
    if (timer == nil)
    {
        // create our animation timer
        timer = [[NSTimer
                  scheduledTimerWithTimeInterval: 1.0/60.0
                  target: self
                  selector: @selector(animate)
                  userInfo: NULL
                  repeats: YES] retain];
    }
```

```
    // show the puck
    viewPuck.hidden = NO;
}

- (void)stop
{
    if (timer != nil)
    {
        [timer invalidate];
        [timer release];
        timer = nil;
    }

    // hide the puck
    viewPuck.hidden = YES;
}
```

Add the **viewDidLoad** method by either uncommenting out the code provided to you in the implementation file or by adding it near the end of the implementation file. You will use this method to reset the game variables and start the animation timer. This is the appropriate place to initialize things, as the view will have been loaded and the view properties (paddles and puck) have been connected and can be accessed:

```
- (void)viewDidLoad
{
    [super viewDidLoad];

    [self reset];

    [self start];
}
```

Run the game and you will see the puck quickly animate off the screen never to return. In the next section, you will add code that will bounce the puck off the walls and paddles.

Collision

The game needs a way to detect if the puck collides with either the wall or the paddle. The good news is there is an easy way to determine if two views intersect each other. The **UIView** class contains a **frame** variable, which is a **CGRect** that represents the position and size of the view. You can use the function **CGRectIntersectsRect** to determine if the frames of these views intersect.

You need to create a function to check if a given rectangle intersects with the puck, and if so, allow changing the direction of the puck into a new specified direction. The new direction of the puck will be optional such that if you specify 0 for either **dx** or **dy** then no change will occur. Insert this above the **animate** function:

```
- (BOOL)checkPuckCollision: (CGRect) rect
                     DirX: (float) x
                     DirY: (float) y
{
    // check if the puck intersects with rectangle passed
    if (CGRectIntersectsRect(viewPuck.frame, rect))
    {
        // change the direction of the ball
        if (x != 0) dx = x;
        if (y != 0) dy = y;
        return TRUE;
    }
    return FALSE;
}
```

Now that you have a nice generic collision function, all that is needed is to check for collisions in the **animate** function. In the case of the left wall you need to create a rectangle that covers the left side of the screen. Creating a rectangle with **CGRectMake(-10,0,20,480)** will create a vertical strip along the left side of the screen. The wall actually starts offscreen at a position of –10 and has a width of 20, which means half of the rectangle is on the screen. You will create a similar wall on the right side of the screen with **CGRectMake(310,0,20,480)**. You can use the **fabs()** function, which takes the absolute value of a floating point number to alter the puck direction. If the puck hits the left wall then the X direction is changed to a positive number. If the puck hits the right wall then the X direction is made a negative number. This will have the effect of bouncing off the walls at the same speed that it hit the wall. In both cases, the Y direction of the puck is ignored by passing in 0. You wouldn't want to send the puck back towards the player that originally hit it. Add the following to the bottom of the animate function:

```
// check puck collision with left and right walls
[self checkPuckCollision: CGRectMake(-10,0,20,480)
                    DirX: fabs(dx)
                    DirY: 0];

[self checkPuckCollision: CGRectMake(310,0,20,480)
                    DirX: -fabs(dx)
                    DirY: 0];
```

For paddle collision, the **frame** variable of the **viewPaddle1** and **viewPaddle2** objects can be used. The Y direction of the puck can be adjusted to bounce off the paddle. If the puck hits the top paddle then the Y direction will be changed to 1, which sends it down the screen. If it hits the bottom paddle then the Y direction will be changed to –1, which sends the puck up the screen. The game should also adjust the X direction of the puck based on where it strikes the player's paddle. If the puck hits the far left side of the paddle then it should bounce off in left direction and if it hits on the far right side then it should bounce off in the right direction. If you calculate the difference of both X center positions then it will give you either a negative or positive number depending on where it hit. Since the paddle is 64 pixels in width, you can divide the difference by 32 to normalize the resulting value between –1 and 1. For example, if the center of the puck hits the far left side of the paddle, the difference between both centers along the x-axis would be –32. If you took the difference and divided by 32 then it would result in **dx** being set to –1, which moves the puck in the left direction. Add the following to the bottom of the animate function:

```
// check puck collision with player paddles
[self checkPuckCollision: viewPaddle1.frame
                   DirX: (viewPuck.center.x -
                       viewPaddle1.center.x) / 32.0
                   DirY: 1];

[self checkPuckCollision: viewPaddle2.frame
                   DirX: (viewPuck.center.x -
                       viewPaddle2.center.x) / 32.0
                   DirY: -1];
```

You should now be able to play the game and find that the puck bounces off the left and right walls and off the top and bottom paddles. You will also notice that if the puck misses a paddle, it will leave the field never to return. You will need to handle this condition and also keep track of each player's score.

Scoring

You need to add a couple labels to the view so you can track scores. Bring up Interface Builder and edit the *Paddles ViewController.xib* file again. Drag over a new label, set the initial Text value to "0," change Alignment to center, and adjust the font size to at least 24. Move the label flush against the right edge of the view. Now switch over to the Size Inspector and change the Origin to the center position. Modify the Y value to be 200, which is 40 pixels above the center line. The result should look similar to Figure 2-11.

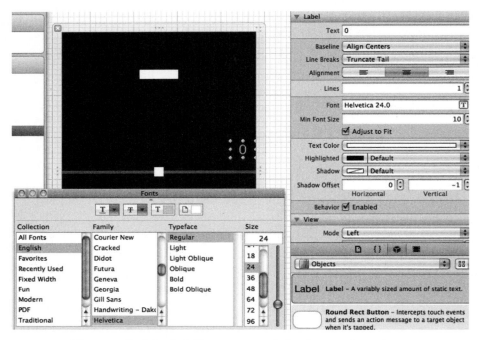

Figure 2-11. Adding score labels to the view

Copy and paste that label and then position it below the middle line at roughly the same distance. Make sure it is flush against the right side of the view and then change the Y origin to 280, which is 40 pixels below the middle line.

Just as you did before, create referencing outlets of the labels to the view controller so they can be accessed as properties within the code. Name the labels **viewScore1** for player one's score and **viewScore2** for player two's score. The resulting interface should look similar to the following:

```
@interface PaddlesViewController : UIViewController
{
    UITouch *touch1;
    UITouch *touch2;

    float dx;
    float dy;
    float speed;
```

```
    NSTimer *timer;
}

@property (retain, nonatomic) IBOutlet UIView *viewPaddle1;
@property (retain, nonatomic) IBOutlet UIView *viewPaddle2;
@property (retain, nonatomic) IBOutlet UIView *viewPuck;
@property (retain, nonatomic) IBOutlet UILabel *viewScore1;
@property (retain, nonatomic) IBOutlet UILabel *viewScore2;

@end
```

You need to add a new function to check if a goal has been scored by either of the players. If the puck hits the top edge of the screen then player two will receive a point. If the puck hits the bottom edge of the screen then player one will receive the point. In order to add a point to the score, you can convert each of the score labels into integer values. The **NSString** class has a method called **intValue** that will return the integer value of the string.

> The **intValue** method always returns an integer no matter what is contained in the string. If the text is something other than a number, such as letters or symbols, it will return 0. If there is white space at the start of the value, it will skipped. It also will return the value **INT_MAX** or **INT_MIN** on overflow.

The integer values of each label will be stored into **s1** and **s2** variables and then incremented by one depending on which player scored the point. The last step is to convert the scores back into strings, update the label values, and reset the round. The **checkGoal** function will also return whether a goal was actually scored or not. Add the following above the **animate** function:

```
- (BOOL)checkGoal
{
    // check if ball is out of bounds and reset game if so
    if (viewPuck.center.y < 0 || viewPuck.center.y >= 480)
    {
```

```
    // get integer value from score label
    int s1 = [viewScore1.text intValue];
    int s2 = [viewScore2.text intValue];

    // give a point to correct player
    if (viewPuck.center.y < 0) ++s2; else ++s1;

    // update score labels
    viewScore1.text = [NSString stringWithFormat: @"%u", s1];
    viewScore2.text = [NSString stringWithFormat: @"%u", s2];

    // reset round
    [self reset];

    // return TRUE for goal
    return TRUE;
  }

  // no goal
  return FALSE;
}
```

Now add a call to **checkGoal** at the bottom of the **animate** function:

```
- (void)animate
{
    // move puck to new position based on direction and speed
    viewPuck.center = CGPointMake(viewPuck.center.x + dx*speed,
                                  viewPuck.center.y + dy*speed);

    // check puck collision with left and right walls
    [self checkPuckCollision: CGRectMake(-10,0,20,480)
                        DirX: fabs(dx)
                        DirY: 0];

    [self checkPuckCollision: CGRectMake(310,0,20,480)
                        DirX: -fabs(dx)
                        DirY: 0];

    // check puck collision with player paddles
    [self checkPuckCollision: viewPaddle1.frame
```

```
                  DirX: (viewPuck.center.x -
                        viewPaddle1.center.x) / 32.0
                  DirY: 1];

    [self checkPuckCollision: viewPaddle2.frame
                  DirX: (viewPuck.center.x -
                        viewPaddle2.center.x) / 32.0
                  DirY: -1];

    // check for goal
    [self checkGoal];
}
```

Run the game and you should see the score increment and the round reset whenever the puck hits the top or bottom edge. You have successfully implemented a working scoreboard, but the game currently never ends. The next step will be to add the game over condition, along with a few more finishing touches.

Finishing Touches

The game needs a few final touches, such as displaying messages when a player wins the game, letting players have a chance to get ready before the game starts, increasing the difficulty of the game on each successful puck strike, and adding the ability to pause and resume the game.

Displaying Messages

The easiest way to prompt the user with a quick message is by using an alert view. An alert prompts the user with a message and requires tapping a button to dismiss it. The **UIAlertView** class is used to display these messages and has a very simple interface.

Add the following to the interface so you can track if a message is being displayed:
```
    UIAlertView *alert;
```

You will add a function that takes a message and displays it to the user. It will also stop the animation timer so that the game will effectively pause while the message is being displayed. In addition, it will not display any other messages by checking if a message was already displayed. Add the following into the implementation file below the **stop** function:

```
- (void)displayMessage: (NSString*) msg
{
    // do not display more than one message
    if (alert) return;

    // stop animation timer
    [self stop];

    // create and show alert message
    alert = [[UIAlertView alloc] initWithTitle: @"Game"
                                       message: msg
                                      delegate: self
                             cancelButtonTitle: @"OK"
                             otherButtonTitles: nil];
    [alert show];
    [alert release];
}
```

You can use this function so when a new game starts it will prompt the user to get ready. You will also create a **newGame** function that will reset the round, set scores to "0," and display the message "Ready to Play?" to the players. Add the following code to the implementation file below the **displayMessage** function:

```
- (void)newGame
{
    [self reset];

    // reset score
    viewScore1.text = [NSString stringWithString: @"0"];
    viewScore2.text = [NSString stringWithString: @"0"];

    // present message to start game
    [self displayMessage: @"Ready to play?"];
}
```

The **viewDidLoad** function would be a good place to prompt the user to start the game. You will remove starting of the animation timer in this method because the game should officially begin after the player has tapped OK. Replace the existing code in **viewDidLoad** to call the **newGame** function:

```
- (void)viewDidLoad
{
    [super viewDidLoad];
    [self newGame];
}
```

The **UIAlertView** will call the delegate back when the user taps a button. If you had more than one button on the alert message, you could check the **button Index** parameter to determine that, but in this case there is only a single OK button so checking it is not needed. In order to handle the alert callback, add the following code below the **newGame** function:

```
- (void)alertView:(UIAlertView *)alertView
          didDismissWithButtonIndex:(NSInteger)buttonIndex
{
    // message dismissed so reset our game and start animation
    alert = nil;

    // reset round
    [self reset];

    // start animation
    [self start];
}
```

The above code will reset the alert variable to nil, reset the round variables, and then start animation. If you run the game, you will now be prompted to get ready before the game actually starts. You will also use this logic to display the "Game over" message.

Game Over

The game needs to have a score that, once achieved by either player, will end the game and announce the winner. I recommend setting the ending score to a low number, such as 3, so we can easily test the game over condition. I usually will use a **#define** so that we can easily change the maximum score value in the future. You will most likely want to increase this number or even make it configurable to the end user at a later point. Add this definition to the top of the implementation file:

```
#define MAX_SCORE 3
```

Now add the following code, which will let you know if the game is officially over. You will convert both score labels to integers and check if they reached the maximum score that we just defined. It also returns if player one or player two has won the game. Add the following to the top of the implementation file:

```
- (int)gameOver
{
    if ([viewScore1.text intValue] >= MAX_SCORE) return 1;
    if ([viewScore2.text intValue] >= MAX_SCORE) return 2;
    return 0;
}
```

Modify when the alert view is dismissed to check for the game over condition. If the game is over, you will start a new game, which will prompt the user to get ready to play:

```
- (void)alertView:(UIAlertView *)alertView
            didDismissWithButtonIndex:(NSInteger)buttonIndex
{
    // message dismissed so reset our game and start animation
    alert = nil;

    // check if we should start a new game
    if ([self gameOver])
    {
        [self newGame];
        return;
    }
```

```
    // reset round
    [self reset];

    // start animation
    [self start];
}
```

You need to add to the check goal function and prompt the user if a win has been achieved. If a win has not been achieved then you just reset the round as before. Modify the **checkGoal** function to appear as follows:

```
- (BOOL)checkGoal
{
    // check if ball is out of bounds and reset game if so
    if (viewPuck.center.y < 0 || viewPuck.center.y >= 480)
    {
        // get integer value from score label
        int s1 = [viewScore1.text intValue];
        int s2 = [viewScore2.text intValue];

        // give a point to correct player
        if (viewPuck.center.y < 0) ++s2; else ++s1;

        // update score labels
        viewScore1.text = [NSString stringWithFormat: @"%u", s1];
        viewScore2.text = [NSString stringWithFormat: @"%u", s2];

        // check for winner
        if ([self gameOver] == 1)
        {
            // report winner
            [self displayMessage: @"Player 1 has won!"];
        }
        else if ([self gameOver] == 2)
        {
            // report winner
            [self displayMessage: @"Player 2 has won!"];
        }
        else
```

```
        {
            // reset round
            [self reset];
        }

        // return TRUE for goal
        return TRUE;
    }

    // no goal
    return FALSE;
}
```

Run and play the game until one of the players has scored 3 points. At this point the game should announce the winner. If you dismiss the message, the game will reset and then prompt you to get ready for a new game.

Increasing Difficulty

It is important to explore ways to increase the difficulty of your game as it progresses. The game as it stands is very easy to play and it is possible that two players may never miss the puck. Here is a list that I came up with that would increase the difficulty of the game:

- Increase the speed of the puck

- Decrease the size of the puck

- Decrease the width of the paddles

- Add additional objects in the path of the puck

You already have a speed variable that resets at the start of every round. The speed variable is also applied to the direction of the puck when it is moved in the animate function. Increasing the speed of the puck every time the paddle strikes it would be simple to implement. One important thing to know is there is a limit on how fast the puck can move, as it could jump over an existing paddle or through the rectangles used for the left and right wall. The paddles are 16 pixels in height and the walls are 20 pixels in width. If the puck had a speed greater than those amounts then it would be possible for it to jump over those objects and a collision would not occur. You will limit the speed of the puck to a maximum of 10 pixels per frame, which will ensure this condition will not occur. Add the following function above the **animate** function:

```
- (void)increaseSpeed
{
    speed += 0.5;
    if (speed > 10) speed = 10;
}
```

Remember the collision function and how it returns **TRUE** if a collision occurred? There was a reason you added that extra logic—it was so you could support additional actions. Modify the animate function to increase the speed of the puck when a paddle collision occurs:

```
// check puck collision with player paddles
if ([self checkPuckCollision: viewPaddle1.frame
                        DirX: (viewPuck.center.x -
                              viewPaddle1.center.x) / 32.0
                        DirY: 1])

{
    [self increaseSpeed];
}

if ([self checkPuckCollision: viewPaddle2.frame
                        DirX: (viewPuck.center.x -
                              viewPaddle2.center.x) / 32.0
                        DirY: -1])
{
    [self increaseSpeed];
}
```

Play the game and notice that after every paddle strike the puck gets faster. See how long you can keep the puck going to make sure it progresses to a difficulty that will cause player mistakes. If you feel it is not challenging enough then you could adjust the maximum speed or add a few of the other items discussed to make it more challenging, such as decreasing the width of the paddles.

Pause and Resume

Games usually support allowing the user to pause and resume an active game. There are a few scenarios that you should handle:

- Screen lock button is pressed

- Incoming phone call, text message, or alarm

- Home button pressed to launch another application

For starters, you need to add a couple public methods to the view controller to support pause and resume. The pausing of the game will just stop the animation timer and resuming the game will prompt the user that the game is paused. Once the player taps OK from the message alert, the game will restart the round.

Add the following function declarations to the view controller interface after the property definitions and before the **@end**:

```
- (void)resume;
- (void)pause;
```

The pause function will be implemented to just stop the animation timer. The resume function will prompt the user that the game is paused. Add the following at the end of the implementation file:

```
- (void)pause
{
    [self stop];
}

- (void)resume
{
    // present a mesage to continue game
    [self displayMessage: @"Game Paused"];
}
```

The application delegate has two callback methods that tell us when an application becomes active and inactive. This is the best place to go ahead and call the new pause and resume functions. This will handle all the events that I listed when the game should pause, including screen lock, system interruption, and pressing the home button.

Devices running iOS 4 or greater go into a suspended state when the home button is pressed. When the application resumes it will still have all of the existing game state, which means the pause/resume logic will work. Devices running iOS 3 or earlier always terminate the application when the home button is pressed. If you want to support pause/resume on iOS 3 devices, you have to store the game state and reload it when the application launches again.

Add calls to the new **pause** and **resume** methods from within the **application DidBecomeActive** and **applicationWillResignActive** methods of the **PaddlesAppDelegate** implementation file:

```
- (void)applicationWillResignActive:(UIApplication *)application
{
    [self.viewController pause];
}

- (void)applicationDidBecomeActive:(UIApplication *)application
{
    [self.viewController resume];
}
```

Play the game and test all the different scenarios, such as locking and unlocking the screen. The Simulator can be used to test locking the screen by pressing Command-L or from the menu by selecting Hardware→Lock. It also supports fast switching so you can press the Home button and then relaunch the app. The only way to test proper handling of a phone call, text message, or alarm interruption is by using an iOS device that supports those operations.

Shake Gesture

I will now investigate another type of input that can used on iOS devices: motion. You already have a good handle on how touch events work, and motion events are just as simple to support. As the device moves, the hardware reports linear acceleration changes along the primary axes in three-dimensional space. You could retrieve this continuous motion of data as a series of x,y,z values, but doing so requires you to analyze each of the data points passed in and create an algorithm to decide when a shake occurred. If every developer implemented their own shake-detecting algorithm, then every app that supported shake would most likely be implemented differently, resulting in some user confusion.

Apple decided to make this easier for developers in iOS 3.0 and came up with the concept of motion events. Motion events use the device accelerometer or gyroscope to calculate the type of motion that has been done with the device. As of this writing, there is only one motion event supported and that is the shake motion. Using this shake motion, as opposed to writing your own, allows the end user to have a consistent gesture that can be used across multiple apps.

When the device shakes, the system will evaluate the accelerometer data for you, and interpret it as a shaking gesture or not. The system only informs you when a motion starts and when it stops. It doesn't inform you about each individual motion, just when the overall motion begins and ends. For example, if you shake the device quickly three times, you might only receive one shake motion.

The first thing you need to do in order to implement shake gestures is have the view controller become the first responder. This may sound familiar to you because of the math game you created in Chapter 1. In that application, the control asking for an answer became the first responder in order to display the keyboard automatically without having to tap it first. In order to use motion gestures, you need to do the same thing, but this time you will make the view controller the first responder and not an individual control. You also need to add a method that tells the system that the view controller can become first responder.

The best time to become the first responder is when the view appears. You should also resign the view controller as first responder when the view disappears. Add the following code into the *PaddlesViewController.m* file:

```objective-c
- (BOOL)canBecomeFirstResponder
{
    return YES;
}
```

Modify the **viewDidAppear** and **viewWillDisappear** methods as follows:

```objective-c
-(void)viewDidAppear:(BOOL)animated
{
    [super viewDidAppear:animated];
    [self becomeFirstResponder];
}
- (void)viewWillDisappear:(BOOL)animated
{
    [self resignFirstResponder];
    [super viewWillDisappear:animated];
}
```

Now the view controller is set up to handle motion events. There are three methods that are used to handle motion events. They are **motionBegan**, **motionEnded**, and **motionCancelled**. This is similar to how touches work, in that a motion will begin and then it will either end or be cancelled. Notice there is not a move method like there is in touch, as you are dealing only with full motions and nothing in between. Add the following functions so that you can investigate how these motion methods get called by logging each of the motion events:

```objective-c
- (void)motionBegan:(UIEventSubtype)motion
        withEvent:(UIEvent *)event
{
    if (event.type == UIEventSubtypeMotionShake)
    {
        NSLog(@"Shake Began");
    }
}
- (void)motionEnded:(UIEventSubtype)motion
        withEvent:(UIEvent *)event
{
    if (event.type == UIEventSubtypeMotionShake)
    {
        NSLog(@"Shake Ended");
    }
```

```
}
- (void)motionCancelled:(UIEventSubtype)motion
        withEvent:(UIEvent *)event
{
    if (event.type == UIEventSubtypeMotionShake)
    {
        NSLog(@"Shake Cancelled");
    }
}
```

Run this in the Simulator and then select Hardware→Shake Gesture from the menu. This will result in debug output that is similar to the following:

```
2011-05-21 16:14:22.196 Paddles[28765:207] Shake Began
2011-05-21 16:14:22.198 Paddles[28765:207] Shake Ended
```

Notice in the Simulator this results in both the **motionBegan** and **motionEnd** events being immediately fired. There is no way to simulate a motion cancelled event, so run it on your device to see what happens. You may notice that the "Shake End" message can appear much later than the "Shake Begin" message. And sometimes you might see the "Shake Cancel" message, especially if you start to shake the device in one direction and then pause for a few seconds.

```
2011-05-21 16:25:34.669 Paddles[7830:707] Shake Began
2011-05-21 16:25:35.273 Paddles[7830:707] Shake Ended
2011-05-21 16:25:36.074 Paddles[7830:707] Shake Began
2011-05-21 16:25:38.547 Paddles[7830:707] Shake Cancelled
```

For the purposes of this game, I think it is safe to assume if a motion starts then the game has somehow been interrupted. Maybe one of the players accidentally knocked the iPhone off the table or somebody grabbed the device quickly and put it in their pocket. In these cases, it would be best if you just paused the game. Either comment out the motion methods that was used for debugging or replace it with the following code:

```
- (void)motionBegan:(UIEventSubtype)motion
        withEvent:(UIEvent *)event
{
    if (event.type == UIEventSubtypeMotionShake)
    {
        // pause game then resume to display message
```

```
        [self pause];
        [self resume];
    }
}
```

You will notice that this code is calling both pause and resume in the same method. I originally created the pause and resume as two functions because of how interruptions occur in the application. Usually there is one method that starts the interruption and another to resume after the interruption has finished. In this particular case, everything is done in a single step, which is why you need to call both the pause and resume methods.

Run it again on the device and make sure the game pauses if you shake it. You may want to revisit this code after the computer player is added and modify it to take a power shot when the device is shaken. For now it will just be used as another way to pause the game.

Sounds

Playing simple sound effects can be done by using System Audio Services. It is recommended that the sounds be short in duration. Here are the iOS guidelines:

- Must be *.caf*, *.aif*, or *.wav* files

- The audio data in the file must be in PCM or IMA/ADPCM (IMA4) format

- The file's audio duration must be less than 30 seconds

You will use this to play back three different sound files for wall collision, paddle collision, and scoring a point. I have already created a few sounds that you can integrate into the game that are available for download from *http://oreilly.com/catalog/0636920018414* or at my website *http://toddmoore.com/*. The files are named *wall.wav*, *paddle.wav*, and *score.wav*. Once you have downloaded the ZIP file, decompress them, and drag them into your Xcode. When prompted, make sure the "Copy..." checkbox is selected, as shown in Figure 2-12, and click OK. The sound files are now included as part of the application bundle and you can access them from within the code.

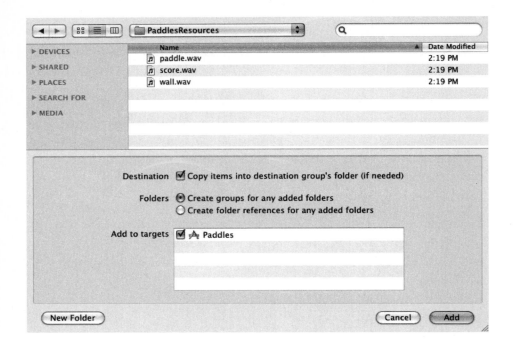

Figure 2-12. Copying resources into your project

You also need to add the AudioToolbox framework to the application. Click on the project file, then Paddles under target, Build Phases, and expand Link Binary With Libraries. Click the plus icon at the bottom of the framework section, as shown in Figure 2-13, and select the AudioToolbox framework. The application should now be able to use the AudioToolbox library without linker errors.

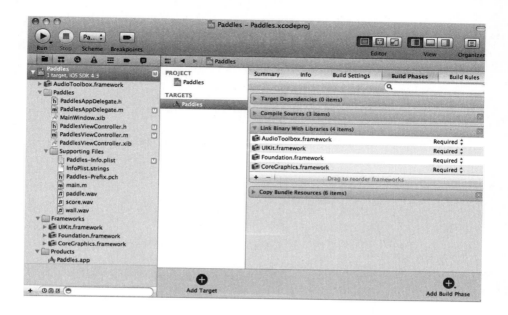

Figure 2-13. Adding the AudioToolbox Framework

Add the *AudioToolbox.h* header file at the top of the **PaddlesViewController** header file:

```
#import <UIKit/UIKit.h>
#import "AudioToolbox/AudioToolbox.h"
```

You need to create an array to hold the a sound identifiers that are given to you after loading each sound. Add the following code into the **PaddlesViewController** interface:

```
SystemSoundID sounds[3];
```

After adding the sound array to the header you need to implement a function that will load each of the sound files and store the results into the array. Add the following to the top of the implementation:

```
#define SOUND_WALL    0
#define SOUND_PADDLE  1
#define SOUND_SCORE   2
```

```
// load a sound effect into index of the sounds array
- (void)loadSound: (NSString*) name Slot: (int) slot
{
    if (sounds[slot] != 0) return;

    // Create pathname to sound file
    NSString *sndPath = [[NSBundle mainBundle]
                                    pathForResource: name
                                            ofType: @"wav"
                                        inDirectory: @"/"];

    // Create system sound ID into our sound slot
    AudioServicesCreateSystemSoundID((CFURLRef)
        [NSURL fileURLWithPath: sndPath], &sounds[slot]);
}

- (void)initSounds
{
    [self loadSound: @"wall" Slot: SOUND_WALL];
    [self loadSound: @"paddle" Slot: SOUND_PADDLE];
    [self loadSound: @"score" Slot: SOUND_SCORE];
}
```

Loading sounds using **AudioServicesCreateSystemSoundID** requires
that you dispose of the sounds when you are finished with them using
AudioServicesDisposeSystemSoundID. Add code to dispose of each sound
from the **sounds** array at the top of the **dealloc** method:

```
// dispose of sounds
for (int i = 0; i < 3; ++i)
{
    AudioServicesDisposeSystemSoundID(sounds[i]);
}
```

Modify the **viewDidLoad** function so the sounds will be loaded before the game
starts:

```
- (void)viewDidLoad
{
    [super viewDidLoad];
```

```
[self initSounds];

    [self newGame];
}
```

Now lets add a simple method to play back a sound from a specified index of the **sounds** array. The playback of sounds can be achieved in a single call to **AudioServicesPlaySystemSound**. Although this doesn't warrant creating a separate method to call this, it has been my experience that you may end up changing your audio implementation down the road and it will be much easier if all playback goes through your own custom function. Add the following after the **initSounds** function:

```
- (void)playSound: (int) slot
{
    AudioServicesPlaySystemSound(sounds[slot]);
}
```

Modify the **animate** function to play the appropriate sound if contact is made with the wall or paddle. You will also play the score sound if a goal is made:

```
- (void)animate
{
    // move puck to new position based on direction and speed
    viewPuck.center = CGPointMake(viewPuck.center.x + dx*speed,
                                  viewPuck.center.y + dy*speed);

    // check puck collision with left and right walls
    if ([self checkPuckCollision: CGRectMake(-10,0,20,480)
                    DirX: fabs(dx) DirY: 0])
    {
        // play hitting wall sound
        [self playSound: SOUND_WALL];
    }
    if ([self checkPuckCollision: CGRectMake(310,0,20,480)
                    DirX: -fabs(dx) DirY: 0])
    {
        // play hitting wall sound
        [self playSound: SOUND_WALL];
    }
```

```
    // check puck collision with player paddles
    if ([self checkPuckCollision: viewPaddle1.frame
                        DirX: (viewPuck.center.x -
                              viewPaddle1.center.x) / 32.0
                        DirY: 1])
    {
        // play hitting paddle sound and increase speed
        [self increaseSpeed];
        [self playSound: SOUND_PADDLE];
    }
    if ([self checkPuckCollision: viewPaddle2.frame
                        DirX: (viewPuck.center.x -
                              viewPaddle2.center.x) / 32.0
                        DirY: -1])
    {
        // play hitting paddle sound and increase speed
        [self increaseSpeed];
        [self playSound: SOUND_PADDLE];
    }

    // check for goal
    if ([self checkGoal])
    {
        // play scoring sound
        [self playSound: SOUND_SCORE];
    }
}
```

Run the game and now sound will be generated any time a collision is made with the puck or a player scores a point. You will learn how to record and edit your own sounds in Chapter 5.

If you do not hear any sounds make sure your device is not in silent mode. This switch is located at the top lefthand side of the iPhone above the volume controls. Also make sure the device volume is all the way up. If you are still having sound playback issues check that the sound files were properly added to the project and that they are being initialized from within the code.

3

Graphics

Graphics are extremely important to any game, which is why I have created a whole chapter on how to create and use them in your game. If one of your goals is to have your game featured in iTunes (and it should be) then you need to make sure your game makes the iPhone or iPad look visually stunning. Apple features apps that make their hardware look great. Do you think Angry Birds would be one of the most popular games of all time if they didn't have cute birds and pigs? What if they decided to save time and money by using white rectangles? No, that obviously wouldn't have worked. When it comes to getting graphics for your game, you have a few options available to you:

- Do it yourself: Create the graphics on your own—and this chapter is here to help! I usually always try to create my own graphics before trying anything else. If it is more complicated than my skill level, I'll pick one of the below options. The more you try to do your own graphics, the better you will get at it.

- Buy it: You can purchase stock photos and illustrations from websites like *www.istockphoto.com* or *www.shutterstock.com*. This option won't cost as much as paying someone to create the graphics from scratch and you may be able to find something close to what you need. I've used this approach on numerous occasions and will typically do a few tweaks to make the artwork more unique. And by that I mean adjust the shape and colors where possible or combine it with other pieces of artwork. There are many times when you will find portions of different pieces of art that can be combined together. It isn't difficult to layer multiple pieces together to create the artwork you had in mind.

- Pay someone: This will probably take the most time and also cost the most. If you go this route be sure to specify before any work is done that you want the original files so you can make changes if needed down the road. It is always easier to make small modifications yourself. For example, resizing an image, adding transparency, or exporting to different image formats is something that is very typical and you should be able to handle it. Working with a graphic designer can also consume a lot of time, so make sure that if you have deadlines that the designer is well aware of this up front and is able to commit to your timeline. A lot of times you end up going back and forth on the design and if you are being charged by the hour then the costs could get pretty high. I always try to nail down a basic design first before any work has started.

Another option that works well for logos and icons is to hold a graphics contest. At the website *http://gfxcontests.com/* you can create a contest describing what type of graphic you're looking for and multiple designers will compete for your specified prize money (typically $100). I've seen this approach used before and it worked great. It allows you to provide feedback to the designers while the contest is underway so they can rework their designs to better fit your needs. It can be a lot of fun and when the contest is over you get to pick the winning entry.

Another option you could try is contacting a local college and look for students that are learning graphics design. Someone there would love to get the exposure and credit of having their work featured in an iPhone game. This way you can get yourself graphics on the cheap and also help a student out by building their portfolio and even promoting their name and website in the credits of your game.

This chapter will show how you can create your own game graphics so you can save time and money. You are going to create a game of Air Hockey, so you'll need to create a puck, two paddles, and an air hockey table to play on. You also need artwork for the application icon that is displayed in both the App Store and on the device after installation.

Introduction

There are lots of tools you can use to create graphics, including free tools such as the open source Gimp program (*www.gimp.org*) and Inkscape (*http://inkscape.org/*). There are also paid tools such as one of Adobe's (*www.adobe.com*) many products: Illustrator, Fireworks, and Photoshop. I have found that the Adobe products are what most graphic designers use and prefer, which may be enough of a reason to go ahead and purchase. This way if you ever need to hire out for graphics, you will be able to keep and edit their work using the same file format.

One of my favorite programs that I use to create graphics is Adobe Fireworks. It combines a lot of the features of Adobe Photoshop and Adobe Illustrator into what I find to be a simpler interface. I'll start the lesson using this program. Even though it's not free, you can still download a full-functioning trial version from the Adobe website to see if you like the product. If you already have another program you want to use then you might still be able to follow along, as most drawing programs have similar features and concepts.

Bitmaps and Vectors

Adobe Fireworks supports editing both vector and bitmap graphic formats. It is important to know the differences between both formats. For our purposes, you will find the bitmap format to be much more limiting than the vector format. So what is the difference?

Bitmap graphics are composed of pixels arranged in a grid. Each pixel in a bitmap can be assigned a unique color. The iPhone screen is just a rectangular grid of pixels. All of the game images you will use in the air hockey game will be bitmaps. However, during the editing process it is much preferred to use vectors.

So what is a vector? It is basically a math equation used to describe a shape. Because it is an equation, it can be scaled to any size without loss in resolution. This is the biggest difference between vectors and bitmaps. If you looked at a bitmap and a vector side by side at the same resolution of the same shape then you wouldn't be able to tell the difference. However, if you were to scale the images, especially if you make them larger, then the difference becomes very apparent. In order to illustrate this, I created a small circle on a canvas of size 16×16 pixels and saved it as a bitmap and a vector. I then scaled both images up to a size of 512×512, as shown in Figure 3-1. You should quickly notice that the bitmap on the left has become very blurry when scaled up, while the vector on the right has maintained its perfect shape.

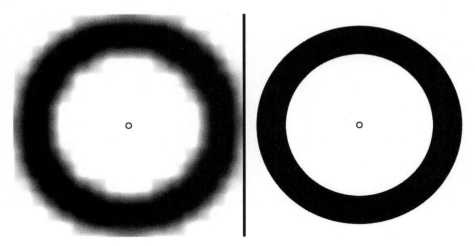

Figure 3-1. Scaling bitmaps and vector graphics

At the end of the day, you will always use bitmap images in your iPhone applications, but that doesn't mean you should keep the artwork files as bitmaps. It is very easy to export from a vector format into a bitmap format. But once you are in a bitmap format, you can't go back into a vector format without recreating the shapes. Therefore, it is always best to keep and edit your artwork as vectors and scale and export as needed.

When I first started creating games, I created all my artwork as bitmaps, thinking I would never need to go back and modify them. I didn't know that the iPad would be coming out and I didn't know that the iPhone would eventually get a Retina display either. I couldn't just scale up my bitmaps, as it would not add any additional detail. So in order to support these devices and their higher resolutions I had to recreate my artwork. This was painful because I had already designed it and now I had to recreate what I already did but at a higher resolution. Nobody likes having to throw away or recreate their work, especially me. If I would have stored my work as vector graphics, then when it came time to update and resize my images it would have been extremely simple. Just remember that it is always best practice to keep your artwork in a format that can scale in case you need to support different resolutions down the road.

Another reason that I didn't start with a vector-based editor was because I already had Adobe Photoshop installed on my computer. I wanted to get my game out the door as quick as possible and didn't want to spend extra time learning something new. It was just easier to use the software that I already had installed, but that kind of thinking isn't the best long-term strategy. I now always create images using a vector-based editor like Adobe Illustrator or Fireworks. However, you may find yourself in a situation where you want to use real photos, and if that case then I recommend always purchasing or creating the artwork at a much larger size than you need. You can always scale the images down if needed and bitmaps always scale down better than they scale up.

Image Formats

It is important to know a little about the different image formats that you can use in an iPhone application. Some image formats support transparency which are portions of the bitmap that are not drawn. Transparency is supported in the PNG format. Some image formats do not allow for transparency, such as the popular JPEG format. JPEG works better for photographs and PNG works better for illustrations, sprites, and basically everything other than photographs. You are probably always going to use the PNG format for your iPhone game, as it is the preferred format on the iOS platform. It is accelerated by the platform, which makes it the quickest to draw. Speed is always an important factor. But sometimes the size of your application can be an important factor.

JPEG is really good at reducing the file size of photographs and will typically be much smaller than the PNG image format. I have used the JPEG format when I needed to get an application under a certain size. Applications currently can only be downloaded over the cellular network if they are under 20 megabytes in size. If apps are larger than this, they have to download over a WiFi connection. This usually isn't that big of a deal but if you find your application sits just barely over the 20 megabyte limit, you might convert some of your larger image files into JPEG. This can only be done for images that do not have transparency, such as full screen background images.

JPEG also is a lossy format which means it can lose detail from the original image. If you open, modify, and save JPEG images over and over, then each time it is saved, the image would lose a little more detail and quality. There are usually settings that can be adjusted as to how much quality the JPEG image will keep, which affects the overall file size. PNG is completely different in that it is a non-lossy format. This means the image will always be the same quality no matter how many times it is modified.

Retina Display

Apple released the iPhone 4 in June of 2010 and with it came a brand new display technology. The screen was the same 3.5 inch size as previous generations but they managed to quadruple the number of pixels used on the screen. The previous iPhone had a 320×480 display at 163 ppi (pixels per inch). The iPhone 4 has a 960×640 display at 326 ppi. Apple calls the technology "Retina display" because they claim the display has higher detail than the human eye can perceive. There has been a lot of discussion whether that statement was marketing fluff or not, but at the end of the day no one can deny the display looks amazing, especially when comparing it to older devices. Regardless of how Apple marketed their new display, it was very clear why they went this route and it was really App Store focused.

Table 3-1. iOS device screen sizes

Device	Portrait	Landscape	Pixels per inch
iPhone 4, iPhone 4S, and iPod touch 4th Generation	640×960 pixels	960×640 pixels	326 ppi
iPad and iPad 2	768×1024 pixels	1024×768 pixels	132 ppi
Older iPhone and iPod touch devices	320×480 pixels	480×320 pixels	163 ppi

At the time iPhone 4 was launched there were already over 200,000 applications in the App Store. Apple didn't want their App Store to become fragmented by a new display resolution. They definitely wanted to make sure existing applications would run perfectly without modification. It would have been impossible to have developers update all their applications to support a completely different resolution between the time the iPhone 4 was announced to the time it was officially launched. The solution Apple came up with was simple, if you want to support the Retina display then update your app, but if you don't want to bother then iOS will just scale your application to twice the size when your app runs. The pixels displayed in your application would effectively be doubled so that it would fill the entire screen and the application didn't even need to know about it.

Apple decided the easiest design approach would be to change the units of the screen from 320×480 pixels to 320×480 points. The difference being that on high resolution displays like the iPhone 4 there would be two pixels per point. On previous devices there would be a one-to-one relationship between pixels and points. Keeping the dimensions the same ensured compatibly of all the applications that already existed in the App Store. Even though Apple encouraged developers not to hard code screen sizes most of us did anyway. Instead of checking the `UIScreen` object for the width and height of the window or querying the `UIWindow` for the frame size, developers just went on their happy way assuming the width and height would never change. Source code was littered with hard coded positions and sizes so this was another motivation for Apple to keep the width and height the same exact numbers.

It's great that Apple maintained backwards compatibility for apps, but now the question is how do you take advantage of this high resolution display? Apple came up with a very simple way to support the higher resolution screens: just add an additional image at twice the size and the system will use it when the app runs on high resolution devices. If you had an image that was 40×40 then all you need to do is include another image at 80×80. If you had a full screen image at 320×480, then just include another one at 640×960. Apple modified the platform to check for the existence of higher resolution images using a simple filename convention (see Table 3-2).

Table 3-2. Image name formats

Standard resolution image	<ImageName><device_modifier>.<filename_extension>
High resolution image	<ImageName>@2x<device_modifier>.<filename_extension>

The `<ImageName>` and `<filename_extension>` are the typical ways that you name an image file. The `<device_modifier>` portion is optional but will contain either `~ipad` or `~iphone`. This allows for providing different versions of the same image for the iPhone and iPad, which becomes important if you are creating a universal application (one app that runs on both devices). The inclusion of the `@2x` modifier specifies an image at twice the resolution over the standard size.

> At the time of this writing, the iPad and iPad 2 do not have a high resolution display. However, with the inclusion of @2x and the device modifier, the platform supports both iPhone/iPad and standard/high resolution images in a single universal application.

For example, if you created an image named *Title.png* that was 320×480 in size, then you could create another image named *Title@2x.png* that is twice the resolution or 640×960 in size. If you included both images in the same location of your application bundle, anytime the application loaded *Title.png* on a high resolution device, it would check for the existence of *Title@2x.png* and use that version if available. Standard resolution devices continue to use the original image file. If the high resolution image is not available then the original image is just scaled up. All this logic is done for you within iOS, which makes it easy to support Retina display and usually without having to write any additional code.

In the following section, you will create two versions of each image to support both standard and high resolution graphics. You will also create a series of game icons for display in iTunes and your application.

Creating Images for an Air Hockey Game

You will now spend time creating the images needed for the air hockey game. I did the following work using Adobe Fireworks for the PC. If you are running the Mac version of Fireworks, it will look almost identical. And if you're not using Fireworks then hopefully you can still follow along, as these concepts should be similar across other image editors.

Making the Puck Image

The first thing you will create is a puck, which just so happens to be the easiest of the three images you need to create. Launch Fireworks and create a new image of size 512×512 and make sure the background is transparent, as shown in Figure 3-2. You need to use transparency because the puck will be circular and in the game you want the air hockey table to be visible in the areas that are outside of the puck circle.

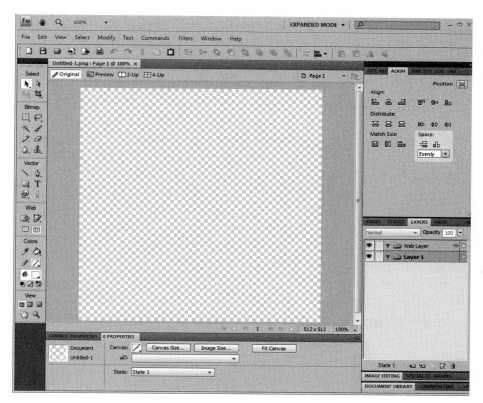

Figure 3-2. Adobe Fireworks

Make sure the Tool pane is available, which is usually displayed on the left side of the window. If you do not see this pane in the main window then select Window→Tools from the menu. Inside the Tool pane there are different groups of tools. Find the Ellipse tool under the Vector group and select it. This tool is shared by the Rectangle, Ellipse, and Polygon tools so you may need to hold down the mouse button on the button to change it to the Ellipse shape. You can also press the U key to toggle between Polygon, Ellipse, and the Rectangle shape tool.

Draw an ellipse of any size on the canvas and then, in the Properties pane at the bottom of the screen, change the width to 512, height to 512, X to 0, and Y to 0. You now have a perfectly centered circle that takes up the entire canvas. Change the Fill category to Gradient/Ellipse, which will fill the circle with a two-color gradient. Click on the fill color and set the Preset to "White, Black"—which will fade from solid black at the edge of the circle to solid white in the middle of the circle. Although this gives you a gradient that is pretty close to what you want, the white is too bright and needs to be set to a darker color. Click on the fill color box, which will bring up a pop-up that lets you specify the two colors to use in the gradient. There are two small boxes below the gradient bar that allow you to change the specific colors. Click on the box located on the left side of the gradient bar. A new color palette view will appear that lets you select the new color. You can use the eyedropper tool to pick up a color or you can type in a specific hexadecimal color code.

> Hexadecimal color codes specify 3 colors: RGB (Red, Green, Blue), with each color represented by two hexadecimal digits (0-F). The color is specified in the format #RRGGBB where R is red, G is green, and B is blue. Each color component value is specified between 00 and FF with 00 being the darkest intensity and FF being the brightest intensity. All the components get combined to create the final color.

Change the hexadecimal value from #FFFFFF, which represents the color white, to #A0A0A0, which lowers the intensity to a light gray color. Now change the ending gradient color by clicking on the box located on the right side of the gradient. Change the value from #000000 to #333333, which will change the ending gradient color from black to a darker gray. The gradient now starts with a light gray color and fades into a darker gray color, as shown in Figure 3-3.

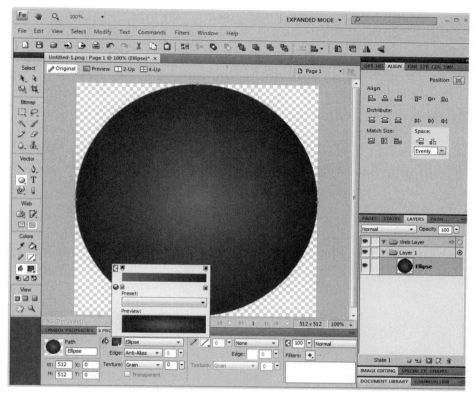

Figure 3-3. Picking a gradient

Now lets add a stroke line to the puck, which will use a brush to draw an outline around the puck. Click the stroke color and specify **#999999**, which results in a gray that falls between the gradient you just specified. Change the stroke line width to 32 pixels and change the Stroke category to Soft Rounded line. Change the Edge to be 8 pixels and leave the location of stroke relative to path set to centered. You will notice that the stroke line is now being drawn off the canvas. If you were to export this image now, it would have the top, left, right, and bottom edges of the circle clipped off, which is not what you want. A little trick that you will use to fix this is the Fit Canvas operation. This operation can be found in the Modify→Canvas menu or in the properties of the canvas itself. Just click outside of the puck object but on the canvas and that will bring up the canvas properties. Click on the Fit Canvas button and the canvas will now adjust so that it contains the entire puck. This is a very handy operation and you will be using it a lot so the image isn't accidentally clipped.

Now you will put the final touches on the puck by adding a drop shadow to it. This will give the puck a little bit of depth so it doesn't look so flat. Click on the Filters add button (which has a plus icon on it). Open the Shadow and Glow pop-up and select Drop Shadow. Modify the distance to 16, transparency to 65%, Softness to 8, and Angle to 315. You will notice that the drop shadow is getting clipped by the canvas again. Just as you did before, you want to click on the Fit Canvas button from the canvas properties. The image has grown in dimensions because of the stroke line and drop shadow (see Figure 3-4). But there is no need to worry about the size too much because everything you just did is stored as a vector, which means you can scale it to any size without issue.

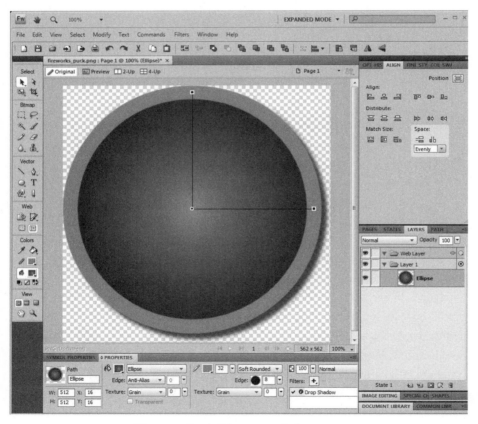

Figure 3-4. The puck image

The puck is looking good, so now is a good time to save your work by clicking File→Save from the menu. Find a suitable location to save your work, such as your Desktop or in your *Documents* folder. I usually store all my artwork under a new folder with the same name as my Xcode project. In this case, I created a folder named "AirHockey" under my *Documents* folder and saved all the artwork there. If I ever need to update the application's artwork, I'll know exactly where I kept the original artwork. It really does help to keep everything organized and under a single folder based on the application name. Name the file *fireworks_puck.png* and click Save. Now you might be thinking this is just a regular PNG image file that you just saved, but it actually contains more than just an image.

Fireworks adds extra data to the PNG file that other applications can't read, such as information on vectors and effects. Other applications such as your browser or another bitmap editor will read the PNG file as a standard bitmap image. However, when you open this file in Fireworks, it will use that extra information to bring back your vector and layer information. So the Fireworks PNG file is really more than just a bitmap image, and although this PNG file would render fine in the iPhone game, you really don't want to use the Fireworks version because it will increase the overall application size. And you don't want the application size to be bigger than it needs to be right? Right.

You need to export the image to a new PNG file that does not have this extra information. Click File→Image Preview... from the main menu and under the Options tab change the format to PNG 32. This gives you an image file with transparency and uses 8 bits for each color channel (red, green, blue). It also includes 8 bits for the alpha channel, which specifies the level of transparency of each pixel. This format is also known as RGBA, and because each channel is 8 bits that gives you a total of 32, which is why Fireworks calls it PNG 32. Selecting the PNG 24 format takes away the alpha channel leaving only red, green, and blue for a total of 24 bits. This creates a slightly smaller file, and if your image is not using transparency then this format would be acceptable.

Click the File tab and Scale the image to 40×40 pixels. Click the Export button and name the file *puck.png*. This is the image you will load for the puck in the iPhone game. You might notice the image file is much smaller than that of the *fireworks_puck.png* file you already saved. This is because you decreased the image size, which in turn reduces the number of pixels needed in the bitmap. You also removed the extra information that Fireworks stores in the PNG file when you export. This is a true bitmap file without any extra stuff and it is sized down to the dimensions you need it to be in the game.

> The Image Preview screen supports scaling the image to not only smaller but also larger sizes. However, you should never scale images up, as it performs the resize as if it were a bitmap. The vector information is not used during the resize operation, which will produce less quality than actually resizing the vector first and then exporting to bitmap. You can easily see this by taking a smaller vector-based image and exporting it to a much larger size. The final result would be very blurry. Resizing bitmaps to smaller sizes will always yield much better results.

You also want to export another version of the puck image for high resolution Retina displays. Use the Image Preview again to export the puck at 80×80 but this time name the file *puck@2x.png*. This leaves you with a standard resolution image named *puck.png* of size 40×40 and a high resolution image named *puck@2x.png* of size 80×80. You will be doing this for all images you create.

Making the Paddle Image

Now that the puck is finished, turn your attention to creating the air hockey paddle. The paddle is actually very similar to the puck except that it will be red and have a handle that allows one to grab and move it across the table. Take the *fireworks_puck.png* file, which should still be open, and save it to a new file named *fireworks_paddle.png*. Notice I am adding "fireworks_" to all the files that include the extra Fireworks data. This allows me to easily find the Fireworks image files if changes ever need to be made. You would never want to start with editing an exported image because it does not include the vector and style information.

The first thing you want to do is change the colors to red. Click the puck object to view properties of the object and then change the fill color. Click on the left color box under the gradient to adjust the starting color. Select the brightest red color from the color spectrum or type **#FF0000** into the hexadecimal field. Now click on the ending gradient color and type **#330000** into the hexadecimal field. This leaves you with a nice red gradient starting with bright red in the center and fading to a darker red near the edges.

Click on the stroke color and change that from a gray color to a red color by specifying **#D90000** as the hexadecimal color value. Change the stroke width to 40 pixels and the stroke style to Soft Line. Adjust the edge value to be 20. As shown in Figure 3-5, this creates a good base for the paddle. Now you need to create the handle.

Figure 3-5. Paddle base

Create a new circle by selecting the Ellipse tool again and drawing a circle that is smaller than the base circle. You will notice that the new circle appears in its own layer in the Layers panel. If you ever need to select this object you can use the Layer pane to select exactly the object you want. This becomes even more important when you have lots of objects within your image. With the new handle selected, use the Properties panel to change the size to 256×256. Switch over to the Pointer tool and make sure the layer containing the smaller circle has been selected. Because of the drop shadow, you will notice that the base object is slightly off center. Drag the handle into the center of the base object, which is slightly up and to the left from the canvas center. You will see smaller horizontal and vertical dashed lines appear when it becomes aligned to the base object.

Now you need to remove the stroke line and modify gradient of the handle. Make sure the smaller circle is selected and then change the stroke color to be transparent. This will prevent the stroke line from being drawn. Now click on the fill color so you can adjust the gradient. I want to create a light-glare effect at the top of the handle, with it fading into bright red, and then slowly fading out the color found right at the start of the base. This requires creating a three-color gradient from white, to bright red, to dark red. Move the bright red color box located on the left side to about three-quarters the way over so it is now on the right side. Then click in the far left spot where the box used to be to insert a new color. Change the new color to white, which is #FFFFFF. Now click on the dark red color located on the far right of the gradient and change the color to **#990000**.

Let's give the handle a drop shadow to give the paddle a 3-D look. With the handle selected click on the Add filters button in the properties window. Select the Shadow and Glow menu and then the Drop Shadow effect. In the drop shadow pop-up, adjust the distance to 56, opacity to 25%, softness to 16, and keep the angle set at 315. You might be wondering how I came up with these numbers and it really is the result of experimentation. I recommend you try adjusting all the different settings so you can get the feel of how drop shadows work. I think you will find that adding drop shadows can take a boring flat image and really give it a sense of depth.

The last touch I want to do is move the white glare of the handle so that it is a little off center. The way drop shadows are arranged imply that the light source is coming from the top left of the screen. It makes sense to move the white glare so that it strikes the paddle handle from the top left as well. If you click on the handle, you will see that the gradient center point, which is located in the center of the object, can actually be moved. This point determines the starting location of the gradient. Drag it a few pixels towards the top left of the object, but don't go too far so that the gradient would be cut off. As shown in Figure 3-6, your paddle should appear as though a light source is hitting the top left of the handle and casting shadows to the bottom right. Even though the paddle was created using 2-D shapes, using drop shadows and a custom gradient has given it a 3-D appearance.

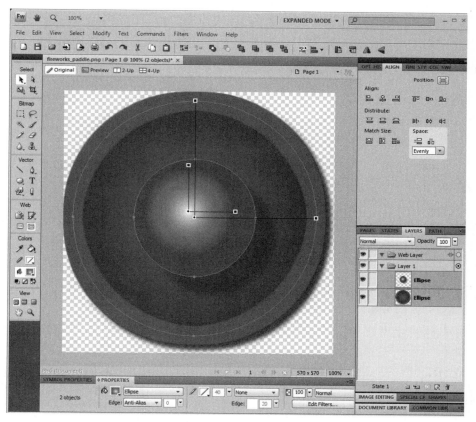

Figure 3-6. Paddle image

Now export the image using Preview Image and set the format to PNG 32, sized to 64×64, and name the file *paddle.png*. This will be the image used for both paddles in the game. Export a high resolution version of the paddle by changing the size from 64×64 to 128×128 and naming it *paddle@2x.png*. Save and name the Fireworks file as *fireworks_paddle.png* and then close the file.

Making the Air Hockey Table

The next step is to create a background image that will represent the air hockey table. Create a new image with a size of 640×960 and set the canvas color to white. You now have a white surface that represents the top of the air hockey table.

Let's create an outer wall for the table by selecting the Rectangle tool and drawing a rectangle on the screen. Modify the properties so the size is the same as the canvas, 640×960, and is positioned at 0,0. Change the fill color to transparent, stroke color to **#999999**, and stroke tip size to 16. Change the stroke type to be a Hard Line and change the location of the stroke to be inside the object.

Select the Ellipse tool and create a new circle in the middle of the screen. In the properties window change the size to 288×288 and position it at 176,336. The fill color should still be set to transparent and the size set to 16. Change the stroke style to Soft Rounded and make sure the stroke location is centered. Change the stroke color to bright blue, which is **#0000FF**.

Now you need to add two goal boxes to the air hockey table. Create a rectangle on the screen and modify the size to be 288×288 and set the fill color to white. The fill color is important because you want to remove the hard wall edge where the goal boxes will be at the top and bottom. This could be done using a mask on the wall rectangle but it is even easier to just set the fill color to white so that the walls are painted over when covered with the goal box. To see what I mean, drag the goal box up to the top and you will notice that the wall is removed as the white fill color of the goal box covers it up. Modify the position of the goal box to be 176, −142. This will put the box half off the screen and half on the screen, which will create a nice opening in the wall. Copy and paste this object into a new goal box and move it to the bottom. Change the position of the new goal box to 176, 814. You now have two goal boxes added with breaks in the wall so the puck can slide on through.

Now you will add a dashed line across the center that will serve as a guide for telling which side of the table the puck is on. Select the line tool and draw a line across the center of the screen. Modify the properties to change the size to 640×1 and the position to 2, 480. You should still have the color set to bright blue and the tip size at 16 pixels. Now change the stroke category to Basic Dash. Open up the Advanced Properties and change the On variable to 50 and Off to 32. This will paint the dash with 50 pixels on and 32 pixels off. I played with the numbers until the dashed line did not intersect the circle and the left and right sides were a mirror image of each other (see Figure 3-7).

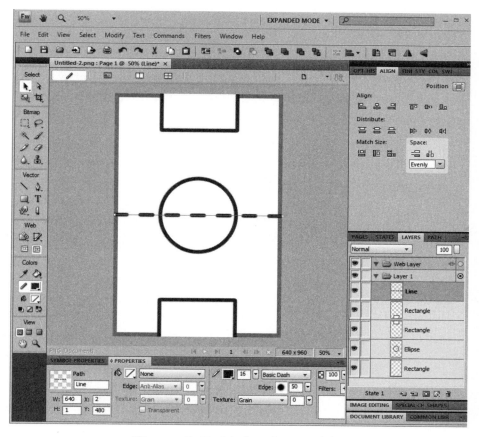

Figure 3-7. Air hockey table

Now that you have the air hockey table drawn, you should export it as a high resolution image by naming it *background@2x.png*. Make sure the size says it is 640×960 before exporting the image. Now export a standard resolution image with a size of 320×480 and name it *background.png*. While you are working within this file you should go ahead and create a title and splash screen.

The background, title, and splash screen will all be very similar to each other so you don't need to create new files for each. You can add new layers into the image and toggle their visibility when needed. Since the title screen will eventually show a series of menu actions, it will be good to hide the dashed line and circle. In the Layers pane, you can toggle visibility by clicking on the eye icon located to the left of each layer item. Click and disable the visibility for both the center circle and dashed line.

Now click on the Text tool in the Vector group. I picked the font "Impact" of size 96 but you may need to use another font if you do not have it installed on your system. I changed the fill color to be white and the stroke line color to be blue. I also changed the stroke tip size to be 3. This will create a nice solid blue line around the text. Click in the canvas and type "Air Hockey" as the title. Put it near the top of the screen so you have plenty of space below it to add menu items. The menu items will come later and will be done using Interface Builder. Now add a drop shadow as you did before with a distance of 7, transparency of 65%, softness of 4, and angle of 315. The image should appear similar to Figure 3-8.

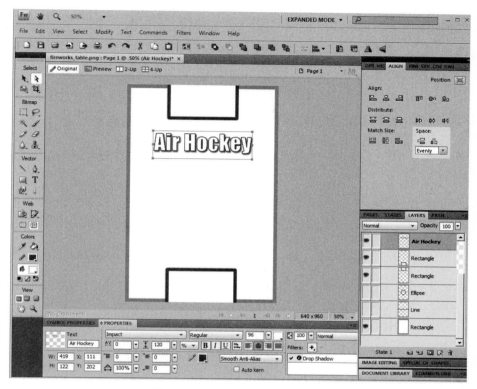

Figure 3-8. Title screen

Bring up the Image Preview screen so you can export this image. Change the format to PNG 24 since the image is not using transparency. Export the image as *Title.png* of size 320×480 and *Title@2x.png* of size 640×960. Now that the title screen is done let's quickly make the splash image. Add a new text item that says "Loading…" into the center of the screen. Change the font size to 40 and the stroke color to black. Also change the stroke tip size to 1 pixel. The shadow will be the same. Drag the label into the center of the screen, using the guides as reference, so it appears similar to Figure 3-9.

Figure 3-9. Splash Screen

Bring up the Image Preview screen so you can export this image. Keep the format set to PNG 24 and export the splash screen as *Default.png* of size 320×480 and *Default@2x.png* of size 640×960. Save the Fireworks file as *fireworks_background.png* in case you need to make changes to the title or splash screen at a later time. The title screen will eventually have buttons that when pressed will allow you to play the game, so you will create that next.

Buttons

Interface Builder lets you use standard rounded-rectangle buttons, but they are very generic looking. It is always best to create your own button images rather than using the default buttons provided. It will also help keep the look of the game consistent, making for a better experience. You will create two button images, one normal, and one hot. The normal image is displayed when it is not being touched, and the hot image is displayed when the user touches the button. Having these two images will provide visual feedback that the button is being pressed.

Create a new file that is sized to 360×88 pixels and has a transparent background. Select the Rounded Rect vector tool and then draw one so that it fills most of the canvas. Leave a little margin around the button. I set the shape to have the origin at 4,10 and the size set to 352×68. You will notice there are a lot of adjustments you can make to the rounded rectangle, including the standard size adjustments, but also the roundness of the corners. In my case, I made the corners as rounded as they could be so that both ends were semicircles. Grab the inner diamond controls to adjust the corner roundness. Now that you have a nice button shape, modify the fill color to be transparent, and the stroke color to be bright blue. Set the stroke tip size to be 4 pixels and the stroke category to be Soft Line. This will make for a normal button that is not pressed, as shown in Figure 3-10.

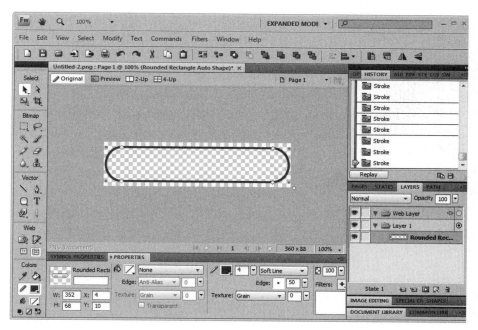

Figure 3-10. Normal button image

Bring up the Image Preview screen and set the format to PNG 32 so you can maintain the transparency. Make sure the image is sized to 100% and name it *button@2x.png* for the Retina high resolution image. Now size the image to 50% and name it *button@.png* for the standard resolution image.

In the layers view make a duplicate layer, which will be the hot button. Hide the previous layer by deselecting the eye next to the layer. Change the fill category of the round rectangle in the new layer to be a Linear Gradient. Change the gradient to go from bright blue to white. You may need to adjust the position and rotation of the gradient such that it starts from a blue color at the top of the button and fades into a white color at the bottom of the button, as shown in Figure 3-11.

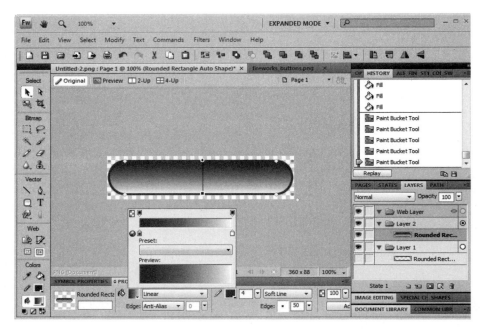

Figure 3-11. Hot-button image

Bring up the Image Preview screen and export the two images, *button_hot@2x.png* sized at 100%, and *button_hot.png* sized at 50% the original size. You have finished creating the buttons so you can save the Fireworks file as *fireworks_buttons.png* in case you need to modify them later.

Review Game Images

You just finished all the in-game artwork so now it is time to double check that everything you created is correct. Review the list of images in Table 3-3 and verify that your images are the correct size (if specified) and name. If there are any images that are not correct, open up the associated Fireworks file and export them again.

Table 3-3. Air hockey images

Filename	Description
fireworks_puck.png	Fireworks puck image with vector information. This file is the one used for editing.
puck.png	Puck image with size of 40×40.
puck@2x.png	High resolution puck image with size of 80×80.
fireworks_paddle.png	Fireworks paddle image with vector information. This file is the one used for editing.
paddle.png	Paddle image with size of 64×64.
paddle@2x.png	High resolution paddle image with size of 128×128.
fireworks_background.png	Fireworks air hockey background image with vector information. Includes splash and title screens. This file is the one used for editing.
background.png	Air hockey background image with size of 320×480.
background@2x.png	High resolution version of *background.png* with size of 640×960.
title.png	Air hockey background image without dashed line and circle. Size is 320×480.
title@2x.png	High resolution title image of size 640×960.
Default.png	Splash screen that displays while the app is loading and is 320×480 in size.
Default@2x.png	High resolution splash screen image with size of 640×960.
fireworks_buttons.png	Fireworks file containing button graphics. This file is the one used for editing.

button.png	Normal button image with size of 180×44.
button@2x.png	High resolution normal button image with size of 360×88.
button_hot.png	Hot-button image with size of 180×44.
button_hot@2x.png	High resolution hot-button image with size 360×88.

That was a lot of work and I wish I could say you were done at this point. But you just have one more thing to do: create the application icon.

Application Icon

An application icon is needed for both iTunes and the application itself. The icon is very important because it is usually the first thing people will see in the App Store. Many times people will just make a judgment call based on only the application name and the icon. Therefore, the icon should convey what your game is about and hopefully pull in people wanting more information, such as the application description, screenshots, and customer reviews. I typically wait until all the in-game artwork has been created before creating the application icon because you can usually reuse a lot of it. This is exactly what I'm going to do to create an icon.

Create a new image in Fireworks with a white background of size 512×512. Drag the *fireworks_paddle.png* file onto the canvas. You will notice the vector objects get imported into the image. Now let's shrink the size of the paddle so it fits into the bottom left corner. You will use free transform to resize the object. Make sure that both layers of the paddle are selected. Click Modify→Transform→Free Transform from the menu or press Control-T. A square outline appears around both circles and you can grab any of the corners to resize. Grab the top right corner and shrink it down until the width and height is about 288×288. Move the paddle so that it is located in the bottom left corner with a little margin.

Now drag the *fireworks_puck.png* file onto the canvas and with the layer selected use the free transform tool again. Grab the bottom left edge and resize it until it is around 180×180. The sizes don't need to be exact, just close enough. The icon should appear as shown in Figure 3-12.

Figure 3-12. Air hockey icon

Go ahead and save your work as *fireworks_icon.png*. If you ever need to update the application icon, this is the file you will use. The application icon is now complete and you need to export it into a lot of different sizes. iTunes now requires an icon that is sized 512×512: when the original iPhone was released you only needed an application icon sized at 57×57. Now with the new high resolution display on the iPhone and the iPad screen size there are a lot more sizes that you should include in the application bundle. Use the data shown in Table 3-4 and export the icon to all of these dimensions with the specified filename.

Table 3-4. Application icons

Filename	Size	Description
Icon.png	57×57	Standard resolution iPhone icon required for iPhone or universal applications.
Icon@2x.png	114×114	High resolution iPhone icon used on iPhone 4 and iPod touch 4th generation devices. Not required for an iPad-specific application. Optional but strongly encouraged if building iPhone or universal applications.
Icon-72.png	72×72	iPad icon that is required if building a universal or iPad-specific application.
iTunesArtwork	512×512	Image used in iTunes, but it can also be included in the application. It does not include the PNG file extension when it is included with the application. Fireworks will always save the image with the PNG extension so you need to rename the file from outside of the Fireworks application to remove the extension.
Icon-Small.png	29×29	This icon is optional and appears in Spotlight when displaying application search results.
Icon-Small@2x.png	58×58	High resolution icon used in search results.
Icon-Small-50.png	50×50	iPad icon used in search results.

Congratulations, you have finished all your graphics work and now can move on to integrating them into a new game of air hockey.

Application Integration

You will start a new project from the existing Paddles application, drop in the images that were just created, and then get everything plugged into Interface Builder. This will be the fastest way to get the Air Hockey game up and running, as you will be able to reuse a lot of the code that was already written for the Paddles game.

Project Creation

In order to copy the existing paddles game into a new project, I suggest using Finder and locate the existing Paddles project. If you already have it open in Xcode, you can Control-click on the project file and select Show in Finder from the pop-up. Go up to the parent folder so the entire *Paddles* folder is selected which contains the *Paddles.xcodeproj* file. Select File→Duplicate from the main menu to create a "*Paddles copy*" folder. Rename this folder to "*AirHockey*" and then open the Paddles project in this new folder.

In Xcode, make sure the Paddles project file is selected in the project navigator. Single-click on the Paddles project name; this will allow you to rename it. You can also do this from the File Inspector in the Utility pane. Change the name from Paddles to AirHockey. You will be prompted with all the items that will be renamed. Click the Rename button to accept, as shown in Figure 3-13.

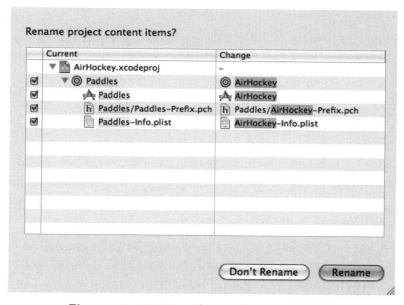

Figure 3-13. Xcode project rename

You may get prompted by Xcode to take automatic snapshots before project renaming and similar operations. This will allow you to roll back to a specific snapshot when major operations are done to the project. I recommend that you enable this feature. You can access and restore your snapshots from the Organizer under the Projects tab.

Now you have a new project you can work with. If you run the application, you will notice that the name of the application has changed to AirHockey. Go ahead and drag all of the graphics you exported from Fireworks into the project. When prompted, specify that you want to copy the images into the project. The project listing should now appear as shown in Figure 3-14. Now that the images are included in the application bundle, you can access them using Interface Builder.

Interface Builder and Images

You will now take various images and drag them into Interface Builder. Open up the *PaddlesViewController.xib* file and make sure the Utility pane is visible on the right side. Now switch over to the Media Library, which is next to the Object Library that you have already used. You will see all of the images listed that were just added to the project.

Before you integrate the artwork, delete the previous game pieces that were created as normal views with a white background. You want to remove everything except the root view and the two score labels, so remove the paddles, the puck, and the middle line view. You can do this by highlighting the objects in Interface Builder and pressing the Delete key.

Now drag the *background.png* image from the Media Library over into the editor. Make sure you do not drag the *background@2x.png* image or any of the other Retina images over. You only work with the standard resolution images in Interface Builder, as the high resolution images are loaded by the system automatically when needed. Notice that a **UIImageView** object is created with the correct size of the image already specified. Using the Media Library is more convenient than dragging over a **UIImageView** from the Object Library, specifying the filename, and then setting the correct size dimensions. In the Object hierarchy pane, you need to move the background image view to the top of the list so the score labels will be visible again. Finally, select the score labels and change the text color to black so you can see them against the white background.

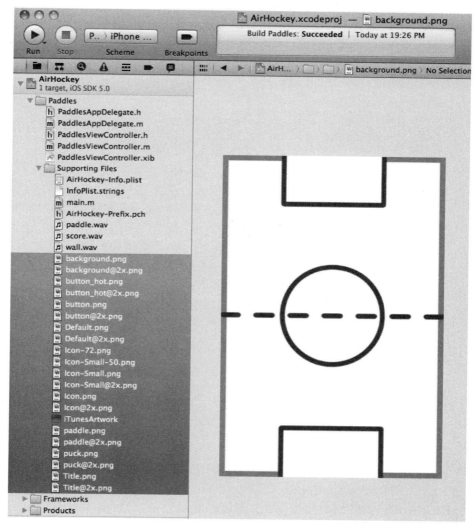

Figure 3-14. Images added into the project

Now drag over the puck and place it into the center of the background. Drag two paddle images over and arrange them between the goal box and the middle circle, as shown in Figure 3-15. In the view hierarchy, verify that the order is background image, score labels, puck, and paddles. This is important so the puck slides over the scores as if they are embedded in the table, and the paddles are drawn on top of the puck if there is ever a collision. Now that all the pieces are laid out and correctly ordered, you can plug the existing view objects into the view controller.

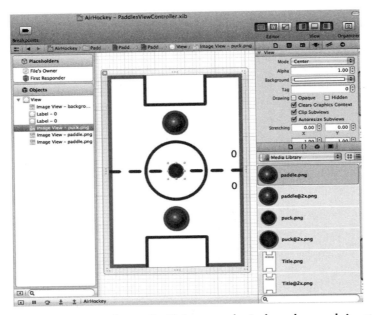

Figure 3-15. Interface Builder and air hockey objects

Bring up the secondary assistant so the *PaddlesViewController.h* file is displayed next to Interface Builder. Control-click on the top paddle and connect it over to the existing **viewPaddle1** property definition, as seen in Figure 3-16. Do the same so the puck is connected to the **viewPuck** property and the bottom paddle is connected to the **viewPaddle2** property. The score labels should still be connected to **viewScore1** and **viewScore2**. Now that you have connected all the objects, the game should function as it did before—but now with shiny new graphics.

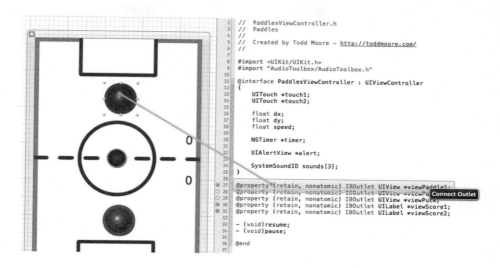

```
 2    //  PaddlesViewController.h
 3    //  Paddles
 4    //
 5    //  Created by Todd Moore – http://toddmoore.com/
 6    //
 7
 8    #import <UIKit/UIKit.h>
 9    #import "AudioToolbox/AudioToolbox.h"
10
11    @interface PaddlesViewController : UIViewController
12    {
13        UITouch *touch1;
14        UITouch *touch2;
15
16        float dx;
17        float dy;
18        float speed;
19
20        NSTimer *timer;
21
22        UIAlertView *alert;
23
24        SystemSoundID sounds[3];
25    }
26
27    @property (retain, nonatomic) IBOutlet UIView *viewPaddle1;
28    @property (retain, nonatomic) IBOutlet UIView *viewPo Connect Outlet
29    @property (retain, nonatomic) IBOutlet UIView *viewPuck;
30    @property (retain, nonatomic) IBOutlet UILabel *viewScore1;
31    @property (retain, nonatomic) IBOutlet UILabel *viewScore2;
32
33    - (void)resume;
34    - (void)pause;
35
36    @end
37
```

Figure 3-16. Connecting objects to existing properties

Build and Run

Build and run the game in the Simulator. You will notice that the animation and collision still works even with the different sizes of the new images. Of course, this is not the game you are going for, but at least it has the look you want. When you run the application, make sure the following things work:

1. The icon is now displayed in the Simulator.

2. Splash screen is displayed when the app is loading.

3. Background, scores, puck, and paddles are all displayed.

4. Switching to the iPhone 4 Simulator shows Retina display graphics. This can be done from the Simulator menu by selecting Hardware→Device→iPhone (Retina).

The graphics displayed in the Retina iPhone Simulator should be the @2x images you created. If not, you should verify that those images were dragged into the project file.

The Paddles game has just been given a face-lift and everything still functions as it did before. In the next chapter, you will spend time improving the paddle logic and puck physics.

4

Physics

In this chapter, you will modify the game logic to improve the paddle controls and create a realistic puck animation. The paddle control logic should be allowed to slide, not only in the X direction, but also in the Y direction. Both paddles should move freely along the y-axis up to the middle line on their side of the screen. The puck should glide along the table with a little table friction so that it slows down after being hit. The collision detection logic needs to work with circular objects, as well as the walls that surround the table. The score logic will also need to be modified to only trigger when the puck enters the goal boxes located in the middle of each back wall.

Paddle Physics

You will start by modifying the game logic of the paddles so they can be controlled in both the horizontal and vertical directions. You also want the paddles to be animated into new positions on the screen so they don't instantly appear wherever you touch. That worked fine for the Paddles game but in the case of air hockey, the speed of the paddle should be tracked in order to animate realistic collisions with the puck. You will create a new class that will help manage the logic and state of the paddles. In an effort to reuse code, you will wrap all the paddle logic into a new `Paddle` class. This object will be used to manage and control both of the paddles.

Create a new object by selecting File→New→New File... from the menu or by Control-clicking in the Project Navigator and selecting `New File...` from the pop-up menu. Select the `iOS/Cocoa Touch` template, choose the `Objective-C class`, and click Next. Name the new object "Paddle," make sure the Subclass is set to NSObject, and then click Next again. Now you can specify the location where you want to save this new file. Verify the location you are saving is the same location as all the other files inside the *Paddles* folder, make sure the Group is set to the same folder where the source code files are located in the Project Navigator and then click Create.

Open the *Paddle.h* interface file and modify the contents of the file to appear as follows:

```objc
#import <Foundation/Foundation.h>

@interface Paddle : NSObject
{
    UIView *view;      // paddle view with current position
    CGRect boundary;   // confined boundary
    CGPoint pos;       // position paddle is moving to
    float maxSpeed;    // maximum speed
    float speed;       // current speed
    UITouch *touch;    // touch assigned to this paddle
}

@property (assign) UITouch *touch;
@property (readonly) float speed;
@property (assign) float maxSpeed;

// initialize object
-(id) initWithView: (UIView*) paddle Boundary: (CGRect) rect
         MaxSpeed: (float) max;

// reset position to middle of boundary
-(void) reset;

// set where the paddle should move to
-(void) move: (CGPoint) pt;

// center point of paddle
-(CGPoint) center;

// check if the paddle intersects with the rectangle
-(bool) intersects: (CGRect) rect;

// get distance between current paddle position and point
-(float) distance: (CGPoint) pt;
```

```
// animate puck view to next position without exceeding max speed
-(void) animate;
```

@end

Notice that you are tracking a lot more things about the paddle than just position. You have to initialize the paddle with the image view that represents the paddle image and a boundary rectangle and maximum speed that limits the paddle movement. The image view will be configured to either be **viewPaddle1** or **viewPaddle2**, which have already been set up in Interface Builder. The boundary rectangle will limit movement of the paddle to a specific rectangle. This will be a rectangle at the top half of the screen for player one or at the bottom of the screen for player two. Attempts to move outside of this rectangle will be stopped at the edge. This object will also move the paddle to the touch point instead of having it instantly appear where the player touches. The maximum speed lets you specify how far the paddle can move in a single frame of animation.

Open the paddle implementation file and add in the following **@synthesize** declarations for the Paddle properties, along with the **initWithView** and **dealloc** methods. This code should be placed inside the class definition, which is between the **@implementation** and **@end** compiler directives:

```
@synthesize touch;
@synthesize speed;
@synthesize maxSpeed;

-(id) initWithView: (UIView*) paddle Boundary: (CGRect) rect
MaxSpeed: (float) max
{
    self = [super init];

    if (self)
    {
        // Custom initialization
        view = paddle;
        boundary = rect;
        maxSpeed = max;
    }
```

```
        return self;
}

- (void)dealloc
{
    [super dealloc];
}
```

The **initWithView** method stores a reference to the **UIView** paddle image, **CGRect** for the boundary, and the maximum speed. The image view and boundary cannot be changed once initialized. However, the maximum speed is implemented as a property that can be assigned at any time. Although you won't be changing the speed of the paddle yet, this will become a useful feature when implementing computer players.

Add the following code to the implementation file, which will handle resetting the paddle position and setting where the paddle should move:

```
// reset to starting position
-(void) reset
{
    pos.x = boundary.origin.x + boundary.size.width / 2;
    pos.y = boundary.origin.y + boundary.size.height / 2;
    view.center = pos;
}

// set where paddle will be moving to
-(void) move: (CGPoint) pt
{
    // adjust x position to stay within box
    if (pt.x < boundary.origin.x)
    {
        pt.x = boundary.origin.x;
    }
    else if (pt.x > boundary.origin.x + boundary.size.width)
    {
        pt.x = boundary.origin.x + boundary.size.width;
    }
```

```
    // adjust y position to stay within box
    if (pt.y < boundary.origin.y)
    {
        pt.y = boundary.origin.y;
    }
    else if (pt.y > boundary.origin.y + boundary.size.height)
    {
        pt.y = boundary.origin.y + boundary.size.height;
    }

    // update the position
    pos = pt;
}
```

Notice the reset method will place the paddle in the center of the defined boundary. This will be useful for when the round needs to be reset and the paddle object placed back into the center position. The position of the image view is also immediately updated to the new location. This is the only time the paddle will instantly appear in a new position. The move method also caps the position the paddle should move to so that it doesn't fall outside the boundary rectangle.

Add the following code, which provides a method to get the center point of the image view, a method to check for intersection of a specified rectangle, and a distance method:

```
// center point of paddle
-(CGPoint) center
{
    return view.center;
}

// check if the paddle intersects with the rectangle
-(bool) intersects: (CGRect) rect
{
    return CGRectIntersectsRect(view.frame, rect);
}

// get distance between current paddle position and point
-(float) distance: (CGPoint) pt
{
```

```
        float diffx = (view.center.x) - (pt.x);
        float diffy = (view.center.y) - (pt.y);
        return sqrt(diffx*diffx + diffy*diffy);
}
```

The distance formula is a standard calculation between two points and is often used in games. You will use this calculation for a couple things. First, you will use it to calculate how far the paddle is from the point it should move to. This will let you know if movement should be limited to the specified maximum speed for a single frame of animation. Second, you will use this method to determine if the paddle and puck object collide.

Finally, add the following code, which will animate the puck into its new position:

```
// animate to moveto position without exceeding max speed
-(void) animate
{
    // check if movement is needed
    if (CGPointEqualToPoint(view.center,pos) == false)
    {
        // calculate distance we need to move
        float d = [self distance: pos];

        // check the maximum distance paddle is allowed to move
        if (d > maxSpeed)
        {
            // modify the position to the max allowed
            float r = atan2(pos.y - view.center.y,
                            pos.x - view.center.x);
            float x = view.center.x + cos(r) * (maxSpeed);
            float y = view.center.y + sin(r) * (maxSpeed);
            view.center = CGPointMake(x,y);
            speed = maxSpeed;
        }
        else
        {
            // set position of paddle as it does not exceed
            // maximum speed
            view.center = pos;
            speed = d;
```

```
        }
    }
    else
    {
        // not moving
        speed = 0;
    }
}
```

The animate function does the bulk of the paddle logic. The first thing it checks is if it needs to do any work by comparing the position of the paddle view to the position it needs to move to. If they are equal then the paddle does not need to be moved and you just set the calculated speed to zero, which represents no movement. If the paddle does need to be moved, then the distance to that point is calculated. If that distance does not exceed the maximum speed, then the paddle view can be set to the new position and the speed is set to the distance moved. If the paddle exceeds the maximum speed then an interval step needs to be calculated to move the paddle.

If you ever wondered why you learned trigonometry in school, you now know it was to animate an air hockey paddle across the screen. The interval step is calculated using the **atan2** function, which calculates the angle in radians between the current paddle position and the position the paddle is moving to. You could draw a line from the current position at this calculated angle, and the position the paddle needs to move to would intersect it. The interval positions that need to be calculated will also fall on this line, as shown in Figure 4-1, and each step will have a distance of the maximum speed. The **cos** and **sin** functions can be used to calculate a position from the origin 0,0 at any specified angle. The position calculated will have a distance of 1 from the origin, which is why you need to multiply it by the maximum speed so it has the correct distance. This results in a point that is based around the origin, but you want a position that is based from the current position. In order to do that, you just need to add the x and y components of the current position to this new position. This leaves you with a position that is offset from the current position at the correct angle and distance. The new position represents how far the paddle should move in a single frame of animation. The view position is then updated to this new interval position and the calculated speed is set to the **maxSpeed** variable.

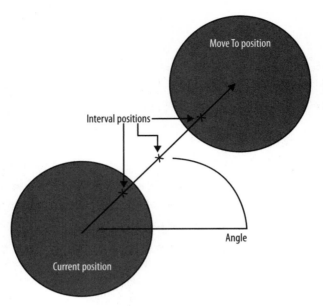

Figure 4-1. Calculating incremental steps of paddle movement

You will now plug in the new paddle object so it controls the paddles on the screen. Add the following to the top of the *PaddlesViewController.m* implementation file, which defines a maximum speed and the boundaries for each player's paddle:

```
#define MAX_SPEED 15

struct CGRect gPlayerBox[] =
{   //  x,  y         width,  height
    {   40, 40,      320-80, 240-40-32 }, // player 1 box
    {   40, 240+33, 320-80, 240-40-32 }  // player 2 box
};
```

In order to verify that I calculated the boundary rectangles correctly, you can add some debug code, which will draw them as red boxes on the screen. Add the following code into **viewDidLoad** before the **newGame** method call:

```
    // debug code to show player boxes
    for (int i = 0; i < 2; ++i)
```

```
{
    UIView *view = [[UIView alloc] initWithFrame:
                                        gPlayerBox[i] ];
    view.backgroundColor = [UIColor redColor];
    view.alpha = 0.25;
    [self.view addSubview: view];
    [view release];
}
```

At the top of the *PaddlesViewController.h* file, you need to import the *Paddle.h* file so the paddle objects can be added into the interface. Create two paddle objects, **paddle1** and **paddle2**, inside the **PaddlesViewController** interface. These paddle objects will be responsible for controlling the two paddles. The **paddle1** object will control player one's paddle, located at the top half of the screen. The **paddle2** object will control player two's paddle at the bottom half of the screen. Add the following code into the interface definition:

```
// Paddle helpers
Paddle *paddle1;
Paddle *paddle2;
```

You may have noticed that the paddle object included a **UITouch** property. This will be used to specify the touch that is currently assigned to the paddle. As such, you can remove the **touch1** and **touch2** variables from the interface.

Modify the **viewDidLoad** method to allocate and initialize the paddle objects. You will initialize them with the views that represent the paddle images. You will also set the paddle boundary to be one of the global player boxes that you just defined. The maximum speed is also specified, which was also defined at the top of this file. Add the following code after the debug code you just added and before the call to **newGame**, as that method will eventually use the paddle objects:

```
// create the paddle helpers
paddle1 = [[Paddle alloc] initWithView: viewPaddle1
                             Boundary: gPlayerBox[0]
                             MaxSpeed: MAX_SPEED];

paddle2 = [[Paddle alloc] initWithView: viewPaddle2
                             Boundary:gPlayerBox[1]
                             MaxSpeed: MAX_SPEED];
```

If the view ever gets unloaded then the paddle images would become invalid which is why it is important to also deallocate the paddle helper objects. Add the following code into both the `viewDidUnload` and `dealloc` functions:

```
// free helpers
[paddle1 release];
[paddle2 release];
```

In order to make sure the paddle objects are positioned correctly each time the round starts, you need to call the reset method for each paddle. This will place both paddles into the center of their assigned boundary rectangles. You can remove all the existing puck reset code, as you will address that later. For now, just replace the entire reset method to be the following:

```
- (void)reset
{
    // reset paddles
    [paddle1 reset];
    [paddle2 reset];
}
```

I want to move your attention over to the touch handling logic. The current implementation moves the paddle images directly to the touch position. This needs to change so the new paddle objects are in charge of movement. The other thing you want to do is position the paddle in front of the touch point otherwise the player's finger would cover up most of the image. I suggest offsetting the paddle about 32 points in front of the touch. That means player one's paddle will be offset down the screen and player two's paddle will be offset up the screen. In addition, you need to store the **UITouch** object in the paddle object itself instead of tracking them inside the view controller. Modify the **touchesBegan** method to be as follows:

```
// handle our touch began events
- (void)touchesBegan:(NSSet *)touches withEvent:(UIEvent *)event
{
    // iterate through our touch elements
    for (UITouch *touch in touches)
    {
        // get the point of touch within the view
        CGPoint touchPoint = [touch locationInView: self.view];
```

```
        // if paddle not already assigned a specific touch then
        // determine which half of the screen the touch is on
        // and assign it to that specific paddle
        if (paddle1.touch == nil && touchPoint.y < 240)
        {
            touchPoint.y += 32;
            paddle1.touch = touch;
            [paddle1 move: touchPoint];
        }
        else if (paddle2.touch == nil && touchPoint.y >= 240)
        {
            touchPoint.y -= 32;
            paddle2.touch = touch;
            [paddle2 move: touchPoint];
        }
    }
}
```

The logic for when touches are moved across the screen hasn't really changed much. You just need to check the touch object that is now stored in the paddle object to see if it is the correct touch. You will also offset the touch position, as you did before, so the paddle is positioned in front of the touch. Modify the **touchesMoved** method to be as follows:

```
// handle touch move events
- (void)touchesMoved:(NSSet *)touches withEvent:(UIEvent *)event
{
    // iterate through our touch elements
    for (UITouch *touch in touches)
    {
        // get the point of touch within the view
        CGPoint touchPoint = [touch locationInView: self.view];

        // if paddle not already assigned a specific touch then
        // determine which half of the screen the touch is on
        // and assign it to that specific paddle
        if (paddle1.touch == touch)
        {
```

```
        touchPoint.y += 32;
        [paddle1 move: touchPoint];
    }
    else if (paddle2.touch == touch)
    {
        touchPoint.y -= 32;
        [paddle2 move: touchPoint];
    }
  }
}
```

The logic for when the touch ends is the same, with the exception that you need to set the touch property of the player's paddle. Modify the **touchesEnded** method to be as follows:

```
// handle touches end events
- (void)touchesEnded:(NSSet *)touches withEvent:(UIEvent *)event
{
    // iterate through our touch elements
    for (UITouch *touch in touches)
    {
        if (paddle1.touch == touch) paddle1.touch = nil;
            else if (paddle2.touch == touch) paddle2.touch = nil;
    }
}
```

You now need to animate the paddles so the paddle images will actually move towards the positions that were set in the touch handlers. For now, you are going to remove all the other logic including the puck animate function. Change the animate function to the following:

```
// animate the puck and check for collisions
- (void) animate
{
    // moves paddle
    [paddle1 animate];
    [paddle2 animate];
}
```

Now let's build and run the application and check if there are any problems. Try and move each of the paddles outside of their associated boundaries, as shown in Figure 4-2. You should notice that the center point of the paddle never leaves the red rectangle. It is restricted to each of the four walls even if you drag outside of the rectangle area. This is exactly what you want. However, you may notice an interesting issue that comes about when you have two players playing at each end of the device. It appears that player two's paddle located at the bottom is positioned directly in front of the player's touch position, but player one's paddle seems to be positioned with a little more overlap under the finger.

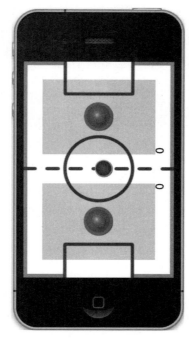

Figure 4-2. Paddle boxes
restrict paddle movement

This issue was first brought to my attention when I filmed the O'Reilly Breakdown video series for *Realistic iPhone Game Development* (*http://oreilly. com/catalog/0636920020639/*). I had just reached this point of the lesson and was testing out the multi-touch with two players. Courtney Nash, my co-host, was in control of player one's paddle at the top of the screen. My paddle was correctly placed in front of my touch point, but Courtney noticed that her paddle seemed to be covered up by her finger (see Figure 4-3).

Figure 4-3. A problem with the paddles

It seemed like it was a bug in the code, so I checked the touch methods to make sure the touch points were being offset by the same distance from the touch point. The code was correct. I then tested in the Simulator and the paddles were perfectly placed in front of the mouse pointer for both players. It appears that this issue only happens on the device. So what was happening?

My best guess is that iOS is offsetting your touch point towards the direction of the status bar. Of course, I have no way of knowing exactly how iOS has implemented touch handling internally but I wanted to dig a little deeper into problem. I created an iPhone application that would help me investigate this issue. The application draws a circle around all the touch points on the screen and it also supports every device orientation. I placed two fingers on the screen just like you would do in a head-to-head two-player game of air hockey and noticed that the touch point was in fact offset towards the top. As you can see in Figure 4-4, my finger-tip on the left side of the photo is closer to the bottom edge of its circle than the other finger-tip is to the top edge of its containing circle. If you would like a copy of this program, please download it from my website at *http://todd-moore.com/*.

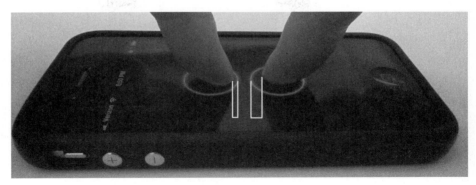

Figure 4-4. Touch offset towards status bar

Another test I did that helped verify this condition was rotating the iPhone orientation into a landscape orientation and then placing my finger onto the screen as if it were still in portrait mode. I noticed the circle was offset such that it was positioned to the left side of my touch, which was in the direction of the status bar. I also tested this on the iPad and experienced the same results. The question now is how can you fix this so that player one can see their paddle? If you could get the entire area that the touch covers then you could place the paddle at the appropriate position, however, iOS only gives you a single touch point so you really have no way of knowing. The only solution possible is to offset the top paddle a little farther down the screen.

Modify the touch method's logic to offset the top paddle by offsetting it an addition 16 points to a total of 48. This appears to be a decent number and you have enough of a margin from the player box where you can still position the paddle against the goal box. Modify the touch logic as follows:

```objc
// handle our touch began events
- (void)touchesBegan:(NSSet *)touches withEvent:(UIEvent *)event
{
    // iterate through our touch elements
    for (UITouch *touch in touches)
    {
        // get the point of touch within the view
        CGPoint touchPoint = [touch locationInView: self.view];
```

```
            // if paddle not already assigned a specific touch then
            // determine which half of the screen the touch is on
            // and assign it to that specific paddle
            if (paddle1.touch == nil && touchPoint.y < 240)
            {
                touchPoint.y += 48;
                paddle1.touch = touch;
                [paddle1 move: touchPoint];
            }
            else if (paddle2.touch == nil && touchPoint.y >= 240)
            {
                touchPoint.y -= 32;
                paddle2.touch = touch;
                [paddle2 move: touchPoint];
            }
        }
    }
}

// handle touch move events
- (void)touchesMoved:(NSSet *)touches withEvent:(UIEvent *)event
{
    // iterate through our touch elements
    for (UITouch *touch in touches)
    {
        // get the point of touch within the view
        CGPoint touchPoint = [touch locationInView: self.view];

        // if paddle not already assigned a specific touch then
        // determine which half of the screen the touch is on
        // and assign it to that specific paddle
        if (paddle1.touch == touch)
        {
            touchPoint.y += 48;
            [paddle1 move: touchPoint];
        }
        else if (paddle2.touch == touch)
        {
```

```
            touchPoint.y -= 32;
            [paddle2 move: touchPoint];
        }
    }
}
```

This problem really illustrates why it is so important to test on a real device. I would have never seen this issue in the Simulator, as there the paddle is correctly positioned at the mouse pointer. The device is completely different than the Simulator, especially when it comes to touch.

Now that you have verified the paddles stay within the red rectangles, go ahead and comment out that code in **viewDidLoad**. It will be good to keep this code around in case you need to later support a different resolution, such as the iPad. It is time now to focus on the puck.

Puck Physics

It is time to put the puck into motion and get it colliding into things with a sense of realism. I spent a lot of time thinking through the best way to handle the puck. The puck logic was a lot more challenging than other parts of the code, as there were a lot of interesting issues that came up along the way. The first thing to realize about the puck: it's the only thing that collides into other objects. The collisions need to appear realistic, in that it bounces off the paddles at the correct angle, as well as all of the walls. The simple rectangle intersection formula that was used in the Paddles game will not be sufficient in determining collisions. The puck and paddles are circular so treating them as rectangles would result in collisions triggering before the objects actually touched and that wouldn't look realistic. There needs to be a little more math necessary in order to properly handle collisions. The puck should also glide like it is on a sheet of ice with a little bit of friction so it slows down after a paddle strike. Finally, the goal boxes require that the puck enter into them to score a point, but if missed then the puck should bounce off the back wall.

Just like you did for the paddles, you are going to create a new object that handles the manipulation of the puck image on the screen. Create a new object called

"Puck" that inherits from **NSObject** just like the Paddle does. Modify the Puck interface definition to appear as follows:

```
#import <Foundation/Foundation.h>
#import "paddle.h"

@interface Puck : NSObject
{
    UIView *view;      // puck view this object controls
    CGRect rect[3];    // contains our boundary, goal1, and goal2 rects
    int box;           // box the puck is confined to (index into
                       //rect)
    float maxSpeed;    // maximum speed of puck
    float speed;       // current speed of puck
    float dx, dy;      // current direction of puck
    int winner;        // declared winner (0=none, 1=player 1 won
                       // (0=none, 1=player 1 won point,
                       // 2=player 2 won point)
}

// read only properties of puck
@property (readonly) float maxSpeed;
@property (readonly) float speed;
@property (readonly) float dx;
@property (readonly) float dy;
@property (readonly) int winner;

// initialize object
-(id) initWithPuck: (UIView*) puck
        Boundary: (CGRect) boundary
           Goal1: (CGRect) goal1
           Goal2: (CGRect) goal2
        MaxSpeed: (float) max;

// reset position to middle of boundary
-(void) reset;

// returns current center position of puck
-(CGPoint) center;
```

```
// animate the puck and return true if a wall was hit
-(bool) animate;

// check for collision with paddle and alter path of puck if so
-(bool) handleCollision: (Paddle*) paddle;
```

@end

You will notice a few similarities to the *Paddle* object interface that you already created. The object is initialized with the image view that it will control, a boundary rectangle to confine the object, and a maximum speed that it can travel. The difference being you pass in two goal boxes which allow the puck to enter in and ultimately score a point. Let's talk a little bit about how I decided to handle the puck implementation.

I originally implemented the puck to take an array of rectangles that represented the walls the puck could collide into. I created two walls for the left and right side of the table just like in the Paddles game. I then added two horizontal walls next to each goal so the puck would bounce back into play if the goal was missed. This left me with a total of six walls that the puck could collide into and bounce off. The Paddles game was fresh in my mind and it seemed like a decent approach. I was going to take it a step further and have a *Wall* object that contained the rectangle of the wall and a new direction of the puck if a collision resulted. Creating this object would let me keep both the wall and collision information in a single object. This seemed like a decent solution, but after I got into it more I quickly realized that the design had serious limitations. The first being, if I didn't make my walls wide enough, the puck could get pushed right through them. This could happen when the puck was trapped in the corner against the paddle. Sure, I could have made the walls wider but it got me thinking that I would really need to do a lot of testing in order to make sure all the walls behaved correctly. The second issue came with the goal box, as the puck would enter in at an angle, clip the edge of the back wall, and always bounce out. It would never bounce in and that was bad because it didn't seem realistic at all. There had to be a better solution, and so I scrapped that approach and decided to start over.

I really liked the approach used with the *Paddle* object, in that you only had a single rectangle that the object was restricted to. There wasn't much chance of a coding error because the logic was so simple. The paddle can't leave the box. Period.

I started thinking that maybe there was a way I could do something similar with the puck. If I used the same approach as I used for the paddles, then the puck could be confined by a single rectangle that represented most of the screen. This would work great to keep the puck inside the table. I just had to figure out how to handle the special conditions for goal boxes.

My first thought for the goal boxes was to just ignore wall collisions when the puck was in between the left and right points of the goal boxes. Basically there would be a middle region down the center of the screen where the puck wouldn't test collision detection against the walls and that would allow the puck to slide right into the goal box and score a point. This was a better approach and much simpler in design than using six walls in my previous design. However, this design had the same problem of my earlier design, in that the puck would not bounce into the goal. The puck would always slide in most of the way but then collision detection would engage and the puck would just appear back on the table when a point should have been given. The design I wanted would allow the puck to hit either edge of the goal box opening and bounce in for a score, as demonstrated in Figure 4-5.

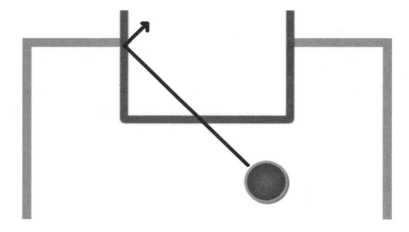

Figure 4-5. Puck needs to bounce into goal box

Along the same lines of having more than one wall, I wondered if the puck could have more than one rectangle that it could be restricted to. What if I had two additional rectangles that represented the goal boxes? Maybe the puck could somehow be allowed to travel from the main table area into these additional areas. So, the puck starts by being confined by the table's rectangle, but if it slides into a goal box rectangle then that becomes its new home. Once the puck slides into the goal box it would then be restricted to this new boundary and ultimately score a point. This would solve the issue of not bouncing into the goal box. The puck could slide in and hit either left or right side of the goal box and still bounce in to score a point. This is the approach you will take in implementing the puck.

Open the *Puck.m* implementation file for the *Puck* object. Add the **synthesize** declaration for the puck properties, along with the initialization and deallocation methods inside the implementation definition:

```
@synthesize maxSpeed, speed, dx, dy, winner;

-(id) initWithPuck: (UIView*) puck
         Boundary: (CGRect) boundary
            Goal1: (CGRect) goal1
            Goal2: (CGRect) goal2
         MaxSpeed: (float) max
{
    self = [super init];

    if (self)
    {
        // Custom initialization boundary
        view = puck;
        rect[0] = boundary;
        rect[1] = goal1;
        rect[2] = goal2;
        maxSpeed = max;
    }

    return self;
}
```

```
- (void)dealloc
{
    [super dealloc];
}
```

You are saving all three rectangular areas into a single array. The puck will always be confined to one of these rectangles. Just like you did with the *Paddle* object, you need to add a reset function that will be called at the start of every round. Instead of dropping the puck in the center, as you did with the paddles, you will drop the puck at a random place along the center line. You can just use the rectangles that were passed in to determine the center line of the table and the goal box rectangle to determine a random position to drop within the circle that is drawn on the table. You will also write a method to get access to the current center position of the puck. Add the following implementation after the **dealloc** method:

```
// reset to starting position
-(void) reset
{
    // pick a random position to drop the puck
    float x = rect[1].origin.x + arc4random() %
                ((int) rect[1].size.width);
    float y = rect[0].origin.x + rect[0].size.height / 2;
    view.center = CGPointMake(x, y);

    box = 0;
    speed = 0;
    dx = 0;
    dy = 0;
    winner = 0;
}

-(CGPoint) center
{
    return view.center;
}
```

Now you need to add the animate function—and this is a big one. This function will handle moving the puck across the table while restricting its movement to one of the defined boundaries. It will also return **true** if a wall was hit. You need this in order for the game to play the collision sound, which is currently the sound used in the Paddles game. I'll get to improving the sounds in the next chapter.

The animate method applies friction to the puck so it slows down if it is moving. To do this, the speed is multiplied by 0.99, so every frame of animation causes the puck to get slower. Initially I had implemented the animate method so the puck could come to a complete stop. This turned out to be a bad idea as the puck could end up sitting partially in the goal box where the paddle couldn't reach it. There would be no way to continue the game if this happened and it would force the players to reset the game, which is certainly not what you want. I had to make a decision: do I write special conditional logic where the puck would always keep moving inside the goal boxes, or do I just always keep the puck in motion? Obviously, the puck didn't start in motion, but I decided that once the puck was put into motion it could just stay moving, albeit very slowly. This worked perfectly and solved the goal box issue. In the code, you will notice I check if the speed is moving, and if so, the speed is reduced, but never below 0.1. This allows for the puck to not be moving at start, but once it is hit the puck will continue and stay in motion until the round is reset.

The direction of the puck is represented with **dx** and **dy** variables just like in the Paddles game. The new position of the puck is calculated by taking the current position of the puck view and offsetting it by direction multiplied by speed. The result is stored in the **pos** variable and used in a series of boundary checks.

The **box** variable specifies which rectangle the puck is currently confined to. If box is equal to 0 then it is inside the main rectangle. As previous discussed, you want the puck to slide into a goal box and then be confined to that goal box. Once it goes in, it doesn't come out. Just like a roach motel. The first two checks are implementing this behavior, so that if the puck is in the main table area (**box == 0**) and is now contained by either of the goal boxes (**rect[1]** or **rect[2]**), then the puck changes the active rectangle to the containing goal box. Once this occurs, the puck can no longer go back into the main box and eventually this results in a score...but not immediately. I'll get to that in the next part of the code:

```
-(bool) animate
{
```

```
// if there is a winner there is no more animation to do
if (winner != 0) return false;

bool hit = false;

// slow the puck speed due to table friction but always keep
// it in motion after initial hit
// otherwise it could get trapped inside a player's goal
if (speed > 0)
{
    speed = speed * 0.99;
    if (speed < 0.1) speed = 0.1;
}

// move the ball to a new position based on current direction
// and speed
CGPoint pos = CGPointMake(view.center.x + dx * speed,
                          view.center.y + dy * speed);


// check if we are in the goal boxes
if ( box == 0 && CGRectContainsPoint( rect[1], pos ) )
{
    // puck now in goal box 1
    box = 1;
}
else if ( box == 0 && CGRectContainsPoint( rect[2], pos) )
{
    // puck now in goal box 2
    box = 2;
}
else if (CGRectContainsPoint( rect[box], pos ) == false)
{
    // handle wall collisions in our current box
    if (view.center.x < rect[box].origin.x)
    {
        pos.x = rect[box].origin.x;
        dx = fabs(dx);
        hit = true;
    }
```

```
    else if (pos.x > rect[box].origin.x +
                    rect[box].size.width)
    {
        pos.x = rect[box].origin.x + rect[box].size.width;
        dx = -fabs(dx);
        hit = true;
    }

    if (pos.y < rect[box].origin.y)
    {
        pos.y = rect[box].origin.y;
        dy = fabs(dy);
        hit = true;
        // check for win
        if (box == 1) winner = 2;
    }
    else if (pos.y > rect[box].origin.y +
                    rect[box].size.height)
    {
        pos.y = rect[box].origin.y + rect[box].size.height;
        dy = -fabs(dy);
        hit = true;
        // check for win
        if (box == 2) winner = 1;
    }
}

// Put puck into new position
view.center = pos;

return hit;
}
```

The next part of the animate method confines the puck to the rectangle it is currently housed in. The puck is confined to the rectangle much like the paddles are confined to their rectangle. The position of the puck is changed to always fall on the edge of the defined rectangle. The direction of the puck is altered to bounce off the defined walls. If it hits the left side of the wall then the direction of **dx** becomes positive. If it hits the right wall, then **dx** is altered to be negative. If it hits the top wall, **dy** is altered to be positive. If it hits the bottom wall, **dy** is altered to be negative.

The puck object is in charge of declaring a winner. There are two special cases where this occurs and those are when it hits the top of the wall while in box one or the bottom of the wall if in box two. These walls represent the back of the goal boxes and if the puck hits that edge then a winner is declared. If the back wall of goal box one is hit then this means player two has scored. If the back wall of goal box two is hit then this is a score for player one. This allows each player to see the puck slide completely into the goal before assigning the point and resetting the round. After all that, the current position of the puck is set to the calculated position and the method returns if any walls were hit.

The collision detection from the Paddles game wouldn't work well because the objects are circular. You need a way to detect when two circles overlap. I started thinking about how to create an algorithm that could detect when two circles intersect. It turns out the solution to this is rather simple. What if you just calculated the distance between each center point and then compared it to the total radius of both? It would basically have the same effect as detecting if two circles intersect. If the center point is less than or equal to the sum of both radii then that is an intersection. If the distance is greater than that amount then there is no way they can be overlapping. The paddle is 64 points across so it has a radius of 32 and the puck is 40 points across so it has a radius of 20. Adding both those numbers together gives us the maximum distance that the two circles could be apart but still touching, as shown in Figure 4-6. Any distance that is equal or less than this amount means the puck has collided with a paddle.

Figure 4-6. Paddle and puck
collision using distance

You will use the distance formula to calculate how far apart the paddle and puck are from each other. If a collision occurs, you need to alter the direction of the puck so that it bounces off the paddles in a realistic way. You also need to calculate a new position to put the puck into so that it no longer intersects. If the puck kept intersecting with the paddle then it might result in a huge burst of speed. That's exactly what I discovered when I started testing. Small hits could send the puck away at a much faster speed than seemed natural and it wasn't until I fired up the debugger and put a breakpoint within the collision check that I noticed it was being called more than once per hit. The only way to solve this was to move the puck so that it was outside the radius of the paddle so that the next frame of animation would not result in another collision with the same paddle:

```
// check for collision with paddle and alter path of puck if so
-(bool) handleCollision: (Paddle*) paddle
{
    // max distance that a puck and paddle could be for
    // intersection is half of each size
    // paddle is (64x64)=32 and puck is (40x40)=20
    // = max distance of 52
    static float maxDistance = 52;

    // get our current distance from center point of rectangle
    float currentDistance = [paddle distance: view.center];

    // check for true contact
    if (currentDistance <= maxDistance)
    {
        // change the direction of the puck
        dx = (view.center.x - paddle.center.x) / 32.0;
        dy = (view.center.y - paddle.center.y) / 32.0;

        // adjust ball speed to reflect current speed
        // plus paddle speed
        speed = 0.2 + speed / 2.0 + paddle.speed;

        // limit to max speed
        if (speed > maxSpeed) speed = maxSpeed;
```

```
        // re-position puck outside the paddle radius
        // so we don't hit it again
        float r = atan2(dy,dx);
        float x = paddle.center.x + cos(r) * (maxDistance+1);
        float y = paddle.center.y + sin(r) * (maxDistance+1);
        view.center = CGPointMake(x,y);

        return true;
    }

    return false;
}
```

Now that you have the puck object, it is time to integrate it with the view controller. Just as you needed to do with the *Paddle* object, import the *Puck.h* file at the top of the *PaddlesViewController.h* interface file. Insert the puck object declaration below the existing paddle helpers so that it appears as follows:

```
// Paddle and puck helpers
Paddle *paddle1;
Paddle *paddle2;
Puck *puck;
```

You need to define the rectangles used to confine the puck to the main area of the table or one of the two goal boxes. Add this code to the top of the **PaddlesViewController** implementation after the existing **gPlayerBox** declaration:

```
// puck is contained by this rect
struct CGRect gPuckBox =
{ // x, y        width, height
    28, 28,      320-56, 480-56
};

// goal boxes that puck can enter
struct CGRect gGoalBox[] =
```

```
{
    {   102, -20,    116, 49   }, // player 1 win box
    {   102, 451,    116, 49   } // player 2 win box
};
```

Just as you did for the Paddle rectangles, add debug code that draws the goal boxes and puck boundary on the screen. Add the following after the existing debug code inside the **viewDidLoad** method:

```
// debug code to show goal boxes
for (int i = 0; i < 2; ++i)
{
    UIView *view = [[UIView alloc] initWithFrame:
gGoalBox[i] ];
    view.backgroundColor = [UIColor greenColor];
    view.alpha = 0.25;
    [self.view addSubview: view];
    [view release];
}

// debug code to show puck box
UIView *view = [[UIView alloc] initWithFrame: gPuckBox ];
view.backgroundColor = [UIColor grayColor];
view.alpha = 0.25;
[self.view addSubview: view];
[view release];
```

Notice that when you run with the debug code enabled, you will see that the goal boxes slightly overlap with the main puck box, as shown in Figure 4-7. This was by design so that it wouldn't be possible to hit the edge of these areas and have the puck mistakenly bounce out. This ensures the puck will always slide into the goal box and ultimately stay in the goal box until hitting the back wall. So did I think about that initially? Nope, while testing the game I witnessed the puck bounce off the edge of the goal box without a paddle being in the way. All part of the journey of writing a game.

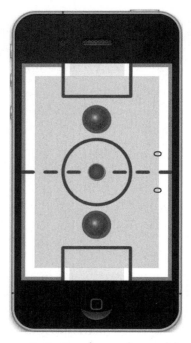

Figure 4-7. Puck and goal boxes

Go ahead and allocate the puck object with the other two paddle objects. You will initialize it with the **viewPuck** image view, boundary rectangle, goal boxes, and maximum speed. Add the following into the **viewDidLoad** method after the paddle allocations:

```
puck = [[Puck alloc] initWithPuck:viewPuck
                    Boundary:gPuckBox
                    Goal1:gGoalBox[0]
                    Goal2:gGoalBox[1]
                    MaxSpeed: MAX_SPEED];
```

Add the releasing of the puck object to the **dealloc** and **viewDidUnload** methods:

```
[puck release];
```

You need to reset the puck position so that it will be randomly placed in the center of the screen when the round starts. Replace the contents of the **reset** method with the following:

```
- (void)reset
{
    // reset paddles and puck
    [paddle1 reset];
    [paddle2 reset];
    [puck reset];
}
```

Now you need to put the puck into motion and check for paddle collisions. Remember that the collision, animate, and goal checking methods return true if a collision occurred, so you can use that to play the existing sounds for now. Replace the contents of the **animate** method with the following:

```
// animate the puck and check for collisions
- (void) animate
{
    // move paddles
    [paddle1 animate];
    [paddle2 animate];

    // Handle paddles collisions which return true if a collision
    // occurred
    if ([puck handleCollision: paddle1] ||
        [puck handleCollision: paddle2])
    {
        // play paddle hit
        [self playSound: SOUND_PADDLE];
    }

    // animate our puck which returns true if a wall was hit
    if ([puck animate])
    {
        [self playSound: SOUND_WALL];
    }

    // Check for goal
    if ([self checkGoal])
    {
        [self playSound: SOUND_SCORE];
    }
}
```

After checking for paddle collisions and animating the puck you will then check for a goal. However, this method is still based off of the previous Paddles game, which will end the round as soon as the puck enters the goal box. You want the puck to go all the way in and hit the back wall of the goal box before signalling the end of the round. In order to do that, you will use the new **winner** property of the puck. Modify the **checkGoal** method to be the following:

```
- (BOOL) checkGoal
{
    // check if ball is out of bounds and reset game if so
    if (puck.winner != 0)
    {
        // get integer value from score label
        int s1 = [viewScore1.text intValue];
        int s2 = [viewScore2.text intValue];

        // give a point to correct player
        if (puck.winner == 2) ++s2; else ++s1;

        // update score labels
        viewScore1.text = [NSString stringWithFormat: @"%u", s1];
        viewScore2.text = [NSString stringWithFormat: @"%u", s2];

        // check for winner
        if ([self gameOver] == 1)
        {
            // report winner
            [self displayMessage: @"Player 1 has won!"];
        }
        else if ([self gameOver] == 2)
        {
            // report winner
            [self displayMessage: @"Player 2 has won!"];
        }
        else
        {
            // reset round
            [self reset];
        }
```

```
    // return TRUE for goal
    return TRUE;
}

// no goal
return FALSE;
}
```

Before you test out the game, go ahead and comment out all the debug code in the **viewDidLoad** method. This will ensure that those views do not conflict with the touch handling of the game. You can always uncomment the code if you need to make adjustments later. The **viewDidLoad** method with the debug code commented out should appear as follows:

```
- (void)viewDidLoad
{
    [super viewDidLoad];

    [self initSounds];

    /*
    // debug code to show player boxes
    for (int i = 0; i < 2; ++i)
    {
        UIView *view = [[UIView alloc] initWithFrame:
gPlayerBox[i] ];
        view.backgroundColor = [UIColor redColor];
        view.alpha = 0.25;
        [self.view addSubview: view];
        [view release];
    }

    // debug code to show goal boxes
    for (int i = 0; i < 2; ++i)
    {
        UIView *view = [[UIView alloc] initWithFrame: gGoalBox[i] ];
        view.backgroundColor = [UIColor greenColor];
        view.alpha = 0.25;
        [self.view addSubview: view];
```

```
        [view release];
    }

    // debug code to show puck box
    UIView *view = [[UIView alloc] initWithFrame: gPuckBox ];
    view.backgroundColor = [UIColor grayColor];
    view.alpha = 0.25;
    [self.view addSubview: view];
    [view release];
    */

    // create our paddle helpers
    paddle1 = [[Paddle alloc] initWithView: viewPaddle1
                                  Boundary: gPlayerBox[0]
                                  MaxSpeed: MAX_SPEED];

    paddle2 = [[Paddle alloc] initWithView: viewPaddle2
                                  Boundary:gPlayerBox[1]
                                  MaxSpeed: MAX_SPEED];

    puck = [[Puck alloc] initWithPuck:viewPuck
                             Boundary:gPuckBox
                                Goal1:gGoalBox[0]
                                Goal2:gGoalBox[1]
                             MaxSpeed: MAX_SPEED];

        [self newGame];
}
```

You should also remove the old variables that are no longer being used from the **PaddlesViewController** interface file. This includes the **dx**, **dy**, and **speed** variables that are now contained by the **Puck** helper object. The **checkPuckCollision** and **increaseSpeed** methods should also be removed from the implementation as they are no longer needed. The *PaddlesViewController.h* file should now appear as follows:

```
#import <UIKit/UIKit.h>
#import "AudioToolbox/AudioToolbox.h"
#import "Paddle.h"
#import "Puck.h"
```

```
@interface PaddlesViewController : UIViewController
{

    // Paddle and puck helpers
    Paddle *paddle1;
    Paddle *paddle2;
    Puck *puck;

    NSTimer *timer;

    UIAlertView *alert;

    SystemSoundID sounds[3];
}
@property (nonatomic, retain) IBOutlet UIView *viewPaddle1;
@property (nonatomic, retain) IBOutlet UIView *viewPaddle2;
@property (nonatomic, retain) IBOutlet UIView *viewPuck;
@property (nonatomic, retain) IBOutlet UILabel *viewScore1;
@property (nonatomic, retain) IBOutlet UILabel *viewScore2;

- (void)resume;
- (void)pause;

@end
```

You have finished up a lot of coding in this chapter and now have a full working game of two-player air hockey. Go ahead and run the game and test it out. You should notice the puck slides across and collides into objects in a realistic manner. This is nothing like the original Paddles game, and shows how you can reuse existing game logic to speed up development.

You now have a game that looks like air hockey, plays like air hockey, but sounds nothing like air hockey. You are still using the sounds from the Paddles game, which really takes away from the realism. In the next chapter, I will discuss how to record and edit realistic sound effects, which will be used to replace the existing sounds.

5

Sounds

In this chapter, you will learn how to create realistic sounds for your game. You can download, purchase, or record the sound effects necessary for your game. Just as it was important to learn how to manipulate graphics, I will show you how you can edit your sound effects and export them into a format best suited for an iPhone game.

What Is Sound?

Sound is a form of energy, similar to that of light and electricity, and is created when air molecules vibrate. You might have heard of the term "sound waves," and that is because sound moves through the air in a wave pattern. These waves are created from differences in air pressure, as shown in Figure 5-1. Think of when you clap your hands, you basically create differences in air pressure, which causes sound waves to be emitted. When the sound waves reach your ears, they are interpreted by your brain, and then you recognize the sound as clapping. In the case of air hockey, we want our sounds to be recognized as those that we might hear while playing on a real air hockey table.

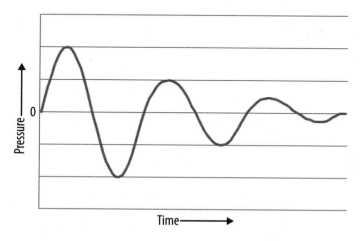

Figure 5-1. Sound wave

Digital Recordings

Sound is recorded using a microphone, which has a small membrane that is free to vibrate. The air vibrations are converted into electrical waves, such that when higher pressure is measured it produces higher voltage. The electrical waves can then be recorded onto either an analog device such as a tape recorder, or to a digital device such as a personal computer. Analog devices convert the electrical signal into a magnetic signal to be stored on tape. Personal computers equipped with a sound card (and they all have one these days) convert the electrical signal into a digital recording. Remember the sound files you added to the Paddles game? Those were obviously digital recordings that you intergrated into the game, but what exactly does that mean?

A digital recording is a stream of discrete numbers that represents an analog signal. In the case of sound, the numbers will refer to snapshots of electric voltage coming from our microphone. These snapshots, if taken thousands of times per second, will give a good approximation to the original sound wave, as shown in Figure 5-2. There are two factors that affect the quality of a digital recording, and they are sample rate and sample format.

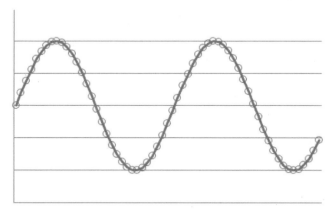

Figure 5-2. Digitized sound wave

Sample rate is how often a snapshot is taken per second. Higher sample rates allow the digital recording to accurately record higher frequencies of sound. The sampling rate should be at least twice the highest frequency you want to record.

Given that humans can't hear above 20,000 Hz, a sample rate of at least double that amount will result in a high quality recording. The standard audio CD uses 44,100 Hz as the sample rate.

Sample format refers to how big of a number is being used to represent a single sample. Remember, a single sample is just a number that represents a position on the wave, and the sample format is how big or small that number can be. The higher the sample size used will result in a more dynamic range with softer softs and louder louds. You might have heard of two common formats which are 8 and 16 bits. This refers to how many bits are being used to represent a single sample. CD audio is stored as 16-bit samples, which provides 2^{16} or 65,536 possible sample values. Using an 8-bit format will reduce the amount of storage space required by half and only provide 2^8 or 256 possible sample values. The 8-bit format greatly reduces the sound quality and I do not recommend using it.

The sound recorder that I use can record in a 24-bit format, which provides 1,677,7216 different values, but personally I can't really tell the difference between 16- and 24-bit formats. There is a much more noticable difference in quality going from 8 to 16, than from 16 to 24. But it is still good practice to keep your master sound files in the highest quality format possible, and export the sounds in a format that is best supported by the hardware. Sounds a little like the advice given in the graphics chapter right?

File Formats

There are many sound file formats supported by iOS. Sound files act as containers for the sound data and include a description of the sound samples so that they may be properly read for playback. This information includes whether the sound data is mono or stereo, the format or size of each sample, and the sample rate. There can be additional metadata, such as the type of compression or codec that was used or even album artwork and artist information. The type of compression used can be lossy or nonlossy formats. You probably remember our discussion on lossy and nonlossy when it came to graphic image formats, and sound is no different.

The source code currently uses the **AudioServicesPlaySystemSound** function, which requires the file format to be packaged in a *.caf*, *.aif*, or *.wav* file. This function allows for the sound to be in either a PCM or IMA4 (IMA/ADPCM) format.

PCM stands for Pulse Code Modulation, which is the technical way of describing how analog sound is digitally represented as a series of numbers in the digital audio file. The important thing to know about PCM is that it is uncompressed, which also means it is nonlossy. You can safely edit the sound file over and over without losing sound quality. This also means that because compression is not used, it will take up the most storage space. IMA4 is a simple type of sound compression that can reduce file sizes by almost 3 times their original size. This can be important if you have lots of sound files and want to reduce your application size.

An extremely useful tool on the Mac is `afconvert`, which converts audio files into many different sound formats. If you are having issues with the playback of your sound files, you can use this tool to create a new sound file that is supported on the iOS device. For example:

```
afconvert -f caff -d LEI16@44100 -c 1 input.wav output.caf
```

This will convert the *input.wav* file into a caff-formatted file with a sample format of 16-bit little endian integers and a sample rate of 44,100 Hz. The output file created will be named *output.caf* and have no playback issues on an iOS device.

You will typically use the PCM format for all your sound effects, and a compressed format for background music. Music can take up a lot of space in your application, and because of that it is best to use a compressed format like MP3 or AAC. In order to play back sounds in these formats, you will need to use a more capable class that supports streaming and compression, such as the **AVAudioPlayer**. Streaming is a good thing for music because we don't want to load an entire song into memory. Instead, the sound file is read in chunks such that music playback is not interrupted and the memory footprint remains very small. The compressed formats can also be decoded with the help of the hardware, which means it requires less from the CPU. The more processes that can be handled outside of the CPU will give your program more cycles to handle other things such as game logic, which ultimately helps to achieve higher frame rates. This is why using a sound format that requires software decoding is not preferred.

Hardware-assisted decoding can only operate on one single compressed file at a time. If you mix multiple compressed formats for playback, every file played after the first one will require software-based decoding and put more strain on the CPU. If you allow iPod music to play inside your game, it receives priority over your application and will receive the hardware-assisted decoding. The bottom line is keep your music compressed and in a format that allows for hardware-assisted decoding to reduce CPU strain, and do not mix iPod music if your game is also playing compressed audio.

Creating Sounds

There are a couple ways to obtain sounds for your game. You can download free sounds from the Internet, pay for a sound effect library, or even record the sounds yourself. If you are downloading sounds, you should make sure the license does in fact permit you to use the sounds in your application. Some licenses do not permit commercial use, so it is important to review the type of license and read over any terms of use prior to downloading or purchasing.

Downloading Sounds

A great website to visit is *http://freesound.org/*, which has a huge collection of free sounds that are licensed under the Creative Commons Sample Plus license. This license allows you to use the sounds in a commercial application as long as you attribute the creator of the file. You can preview sounds directly from the website, but if you want to download the file you will need to create a free account. This also works nicely because the website tracks every sound file you download, which helps you to properly give credit to the person who created the sound. This website does not include songs or compositions, so if you want that in your game you will have to look elsewhere.

One of my favorite ways to create music is using GarageBand that comes free on Mac OS X. It includes many loops that can be used in your game. You can also use the audition feature to pick a genre of music and select different types of instruments that you want in your song. It will create a starter song for you that you can edit and make unique. It can be a lot of fun, and I recommend trying that if you're looking for a decent free option for music or background beats. I used a few trance-style loops from Garage Band in my Glow Burst game. The loops were small enough that they could be loaded into memory using OpenAL, which allowed me to dynamically change the pitch of the sound. This allowed me to speed the music up as time elapsed, adding a little more intensity to the game. The player not only had the pressure of watching a timer bar but also could hear it with the music speeding up.

> OpenAL stands for Open Audio Library and is a cross-platform sound API that is supported on all iOS devices. It supports mixing multiple sounds together, three-dimensional positioning of sounds, and even adjusting pitch and other characteristics. OpenAL is a great library to use when you need total control over the playback of sounds.

Another option for getting music into your game is purchasing royalty-free music. The websites *http://www.partnersinrhyme.com/* and *http://www.musicloops .com/* have a large selection of music available at reasonable rates. Those sites also have a very flexible license agreement, but as always be sure to read over the restrictions to make sure the license will meet your needs.

Recording Sounds

In order to create your own sounds of air hockey you will need a digital sound recorder or a microphone connected directly to your computer. You will also need a couple of props. In my case, I had a friend let me borrow their air hockey table pieces, which included two paddles and a puck. If you don't have these items available, you could always use something similar such as a coffee mug for the paddle, and a hard plastic coaster for the puck. You just need objects that will make similar sounds.

One of my apps that I thought had really good sounds was called App Ocean. This was a physics simulation where apps drop into an ocean. You hear them splash in, and you also hear them hit the bottom of the ocean and other apps. In order to create those sound effects, I recorded dice dropping into a cup of water. You heard the splash of the water, and then you heard the collision when it hit the bottom of the cup. It worked out really well and only took a couple minutes of my time to record. Another common sound effect you might need are guns and explosions. I once brought my recorder to a gun range and just left it recording on a table. It captured a lot of different sounds that I can use as is, or after applying effects such as pitch shifting—which I used to morph gunshot sounds into powerful explosions. It can be a lot of fun creating your own sounds, and even give you an excuse to get out of the house.

When it comes time to actually do the sound recording, make sure you do so in a quiet place if possible. Always leave at least a second of silence before and after the recording. I will show you how to trim away this silence in a bit but just remember the microphone can actually "hear" better than your ears can. This is why it is important not to turn off the recording too early, and even more important to make sure nobody is talking and minimize the use of noisy equipment. My recorder picks up so much ambient noise that I sometimes have to turn off things like the house air conditioner or shut down computers that have a noisy fan. Take a recording of complete silence and give it a listen to see if there is any noise in the playback. You can then make adjustments to make it as quiet as possible.

I suggest picking up a basic field recorder to do your recordings. That way you will be mobile and can easily get the microphone into the best position. On the set of the O'Reilly Breakdown series, I used my field recorder with the help of Courtney Nash to record the paddle sounds (see Figure 5-3). Make sure to configure your recorder so that the recording will be done with at least a 44 kHz sample rate and 16-bit sound format. This is the same format you will find with CD audio. Most recording devices or software will record in the best possible format so you might not even have to make adjustments. The most important part of recording is watching your levels. Distortion can be created if your levels get too high or go above the maximum level. The other issue is the level being too soft, as that will add a lot of noise especially when you normalize the sound (we will discuss normalization later).

Figure 5-3. Recording sounds

You want to record three sounds for the air hockey game:

- The puck hitting the wall

- The paddle striking the puck

- The puck dropping into the goal

Start the recorder and place the microphone or device on the table so you can record the game objects. We will record the sound of the puck hitting the wall. Take the puck, coaster, or whatever you're using to represent the puck and tap it on the table a few times. Make sure to get pretty close to the microphone, but keep a close eye on the levels, as you don't want it to be so close that it distorts. Record this sound multiple times, each at a slightly different angle and position. You want a lot of different options so you can pick the best one to use during the edit process. Take the paddle object and slide it into the puck such that the puck slides away from the microphone. Again, take a few recordings so you have options, and make sure not to make any noise before or after the recording. The sound effect should be a nice smooth sliding sound that fades away from the microphone. Now drop the puck on the table at an angle so hopefully it spins around before coming to a stop. This will be the score sound when the puck drops into the goal. As before, make sure to record multiple versions so you can pick the best one.

Once you have recorded all three sounds each with several variations you can stop the recording. Transferring the sound files to the computer is usually accomplished by connecting the supplied USB cable from the device to the computer and accessing it like an external drive. If you used a software program to record your sounds, make sure to save a backup copy so you can always revert to the original if needed. If you are prompted to pick a sound format to save in, always choose a nonlossy format such as uncompressed PCM. Never use a lossy format such as MP3 to save your master recording.

You will now learn how to edit this recording into three short sound effects for use in the game.

Editing Sounds

In this section, you will use Audacity, which is an open source tool for recording and editing sounds. Download a free copy of Audacity at *http://audacity.sourceforge.net/*, which can be installed on Windows, Mac OS X, and Linux operating systems. I will show you how to use Audacity to crop, trim, normalize, and fade out each sound effect.

I always keep a master copy of my sound recording that will never be modified. This allows you to start over during the editing process. The first thing you need to do is make a copy of your master audio file and open it with Audacity. You will now be presented with a graph of your wave form audio. Put on a set of headphones and listen to your audio. It is important to use headphones instead of listening with speakers because you will be able to hear things much clearer. I have made the mistake of just using desktop speakers—it can lead to mistakes in editing, or leaving in background noise that can only be heard with headphones. We want our sound to not include any unwanted noises such as people talking, pops, or distortion.

As shown in Figure 5-4, I highlighted the sound that I found the most pleasing for the score sound effect. I could hear the puck land on the table and roll around along the edges and it sounded great. It also looks great in terms of the graph, as it was uniform and had good levels. It wasn't too loud where it would distort, and not too low where you could hear other noise. Once you have isolated your favorite scoring sound, change the selection to all the audio before it starts. Make sure to keep a little bit of silence before the sound starts and either hit the Delete key or select Edit→Delete from the menu. Press the play button from the toolbar or the space key to hear the sound from the beginning, which should start with the sound you wanted. Now select right before the next sound starts, leaving plenty of silence after the clip, and highlight all the way to the end. Press Delete again and you will have our sound effect completely isolated with silence padded on both ends. Press Command-F or select View→Fit in Window so that the entire clip will fill the window, making it easier to see the sound data points. At this point you should be able to play the sound and it will be the only sound effect heard. There should be plenty of silence such that the clip does not abruptly stop during the playback. If you trimmed too close to the sound you can also undo your edits and try again, using Command-Z or selecting Edit→Undo from the menu.

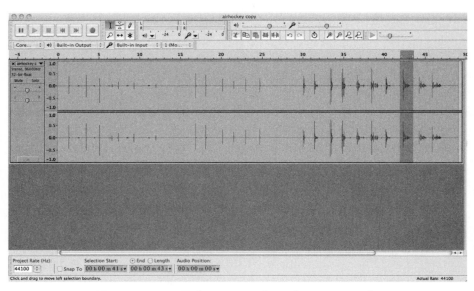

Figure 5-4. Editing air hockey sounds

You want the audio to play immediately, which means you need to really dig into the start of the sound and delete as much as possible. A simple way to do this is by selecting the first portion of the sound and pressing Command-E to zoom in to the entire selection, or by selecting View→Zoom to Selection from the menu. I suggest doing this a few times until you can zoom in far enough to see both silence and the start of the audio wave, as shown in Figure 5-5. If you cut into the sound too much, it might create a popping sound since the sound wave would not flow smoothly from the start. Place the cursor on top of silence but pretty close to the start of the audio. Now select Edit→Select Left of Playback Position from the menu. You will be prompted to specify where to select, which you should leave set to 0 hours, 0 minutes, 0 seconds to specify the start. Click OK and now all the audio before the cursor will be selected. Press the Delete key to remove this audio. Now press Command-F to fit the entire sound clip in the window.

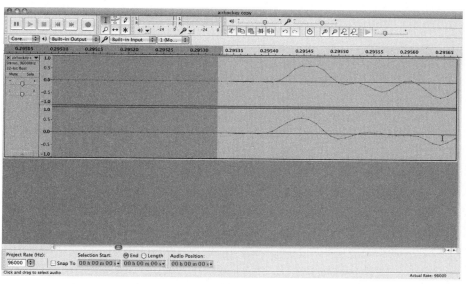

Figure 5-5. Highlighting audio to delete

Play the audio back so you can determine where the sound stops and silence begins. In my case, it was around the one second mark, which is a good length for this sound effect. I selected everything from this position to the end and then deleted it. The sound clip was left completely isolated and trimmed, which provides for quicker playback. Just to make sure the clip ends on silence, highlight a portion of the audio near the end and select Edit→Fade Out from the menu, as shown in Figure

5-6. This will make sure the sound does not abruptly stop but rather smoothly fades away. In my case, I ended up selecting about 0.25 seconds of audio at the end to fade out. There is no hard rule on what works best, so you might want to try a few different durations. The goal is to always start the sound effect as quickly as possible from silence, and then fade out the sound near the end so no artifacts exist.

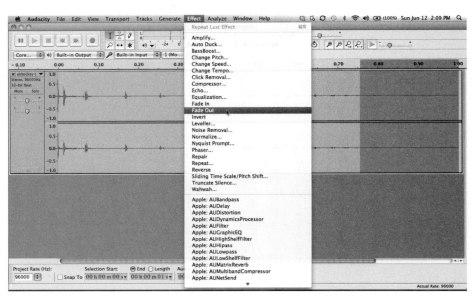

Figure 5-6. Fading out the audio

The final touch you want to do is normalize the audio. This will make sure all of our sound effects are of the same sound level. It would be great if all our recordings had the same levels, but it is impractical to think you can achieve that in the recording process alone. Normalizing your audio will make the levels peak to the same amount, which will keep all of the sound effects consistant across the board. The entire sound clip will be scaled to a new maximum amount. Select Effect→Normalize from the menu, which will prompt you to specify the maximum amplitude. I recommend using something less than the maximum amount of 0 dB. Change the maximum amplitude to be −1 dB, as shown in Figure 5-7. This will give a little headroom that should help out if this sound ever needs to be mixed with others. For now, you just want all the sounds to have the same maximum level.

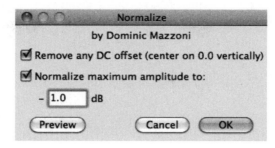

Figure 5-7. Normalizing audio

Now you need to export the sound so it can be used by the game. Select File→Export from the menu and save the file format to be a WAV-signed 16-bit PCM. Now repeat all these steps for our paddle and wall collisions. Verify that all the files you exported are named *score.wav*, *wall.wav*, and *paddle.wav*. Open each of them in Audacity and verify they are in the proper format and are fairly short in length.

You have finished recording and editing the sounds necessary for the air hockey game. Now you just need to copy and replace the existing sounds from our Paddles game into our Air Hockey project. You will need to use Finder to copy and replace the existing sound files. You can quickly open Finder to the existing sounds by Command-clicking on one of the sound files in the project, and selecting Show in Finder from the pop-up. Build and run the game with the new sounds and make sure they all play back correctly. You might need to do a clean build in case the previous sounds were not updated during the build process. Hopefully you will find that the game looks, plays, and now sounds realistic.

6

Computer AI

In this chapter, I will show how to create a computer player that can play a decent game of air hockey. I will investigate the different behaviors of a human player in order to come up with a strategy that the computer can follow. This logic will tweaked to allow for different difficulty levels of play. Multiple levels of play will allow people to start at an easier level so they can learn how to play and then progress up in difficulty. The first thing you will need to do is create a title screen for the game so the player can choose to play against the computer or play the two player mode that has already been implemented.

Computer Player Menu

You have only been using one view controller that is in charge of the gameplay. You will now introduce a new view controller to manage the title screen. You need to create a new view controller just like you did for the *Paddle* and *Puck* objects, by Control-clicking the *Paddles* folder in the Navigator and selecting New File... from the pop-up menu. Instead of selecting the `NSObject` subclass, you will select `UIViewController` instead, and then click Next. Name the Class `TitleViewController`, make sure the "Targeted for iPad" option is not checked, "With XIB for user interface" is checked, and then click Next. Make sure the new class is being created in the same location as all the other files and click Create. Xcode has created *TitleViewController.h*, *TitleViewController.m*, and *TitleViewController.xib* files and added them to the project.

You will now design the title view by using the title image that you created in Chapter 3, the Graphics chapter, along with buttons to select between two player or computer mode. Select the *TitleViewController.xib* file in the Project Navigator to display the file in the Interface Builder editor. Make sure the Utility pane is open so you can get access to the inspectors, and then select the Attributes Inspector. As you did with the Paddles game, change the Status Bar under Simulated Metrics to None. Click on the Size Inspector and adjust the view height to be 480, which represents the full screen without the status bar. Using the Media Library, drag over the *Title.png* file into the main view. Align the image view so that it fills the entire view. Switch over to the Objects Library and drag two Round Rect Buttons onto the view and position them into the center of the screen. Change the button text on the top button to "Computer" and the bottom button to "Two Player." Change both button sizes to be 180×44, which match the button image sizes you created in Chapter 3, the Graphics chapter. The default buttons will appear as shown in Figure 6-1.

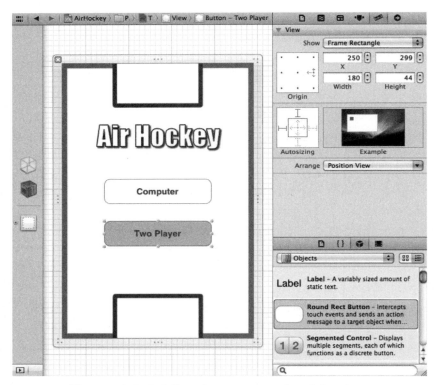

Figure 6-1. Adding buttons to the title view

Buttons will always be in one of four different states: normal, highlight, selected, and disabled. The button properties such as title text, title color, and background image are set to a specific button state. The buttons that you already created represent the normal and highlighted states. The other states, selected and disabled, are not going to be used. The selected state only really applies to segment controls where you have selected a specific item that will remain selected until you change it. The disabled state does not allow for the button to be pressed and will typically be grayed out to show this. The buttons on the title screen will never be disabled so this state is also not needed.

Select both of the buttons by clicking on the Computer button, then press and hold the Command button while clicking on the Two Player button. Now that both buttons are selected, you can edit their properties at the same time. Change the Type of button to Custom. With the State Config set to Default, change the Background image dropdown to *button.png*. You will leave the Text Color set to the default blue color. Now switch the State Config to Highlighted, and change the Background image to *button_hot.png*. The Text Color of the button should stay White Color for the Highlighted state so it can be easily read against the blue gradient background. The buttons should now appear with the background of the *button.png* image, as shown in Figure 6-2. The title view, when displayed, will toggle between the two button images when tapped.

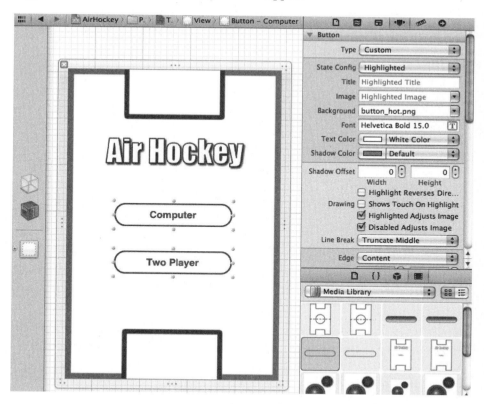

Figure 6-2. Buttons with images

Create a new action outlet from the Two Player button to the `TitleView Controller` header file and name the new method `onPlay`. You could create a new function for the Computer button, but I'd rather use the Tag property to pass along an integer value to the same method. The only thing you really need to tell the view controller is if the computer should be playing or not. So you can just set the Tag variable to specify if the computer is playing or not. A value of 0 will mean that the computer is not playing and a value of 1 means the computer is playing. In order to do this, create an action from the Computer button to the existing `onPlay` method as shown in Figure 6-3.

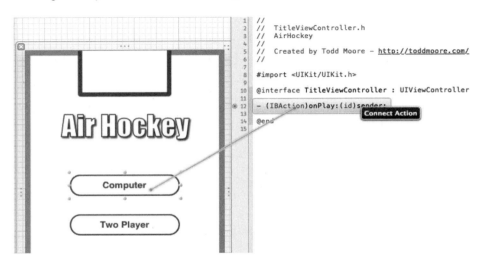

Figure 6-3. Connecting action to existing method

Bring up the Attributes Inspector for the Computer button and enter a value of 1 for the Tag property, as shown in Figure 6-4. The default tag value is 0, which means the Two Player button is already good to go. The `onPlay` method passes along the sending control when it is tapped, so you can use that parameter to query for the Tag value. This will allow you to know which button was pressed, based on the Tag number, while reusing the same method to handle starting the game.

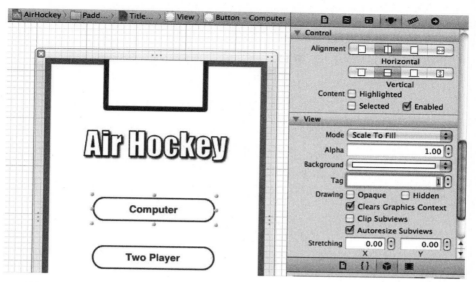

Figure 6-4. Specifying Tag number in Interface Builder

Now you need to change the app to launch the new title view controller instead of the previous game controller. The application delegate is responsible for creating the **PaddlesViewController** and assigning it to the **viewController** property. You want to modify it such that the **TitleViewController** is created initially instead of the **PaddlesViewController**.

You need to update the *PaddlesAppDelegate.h* file to use the **TitleView Controller** class. In order to do this, you need to add a class declaration under the existing **PaddlesViewController** declaration so that it appears as follows:

```
#import <UIKit/UIKit.h>

@class PaddlesViewController;
@class TitleViewController;
```

Now change the **viewController** property from a **PaddlesViewController** to a **TitleViewController**, so that it appears as follows:

```
@property (strong, nonatomic) TitleViewController
*viewController;
```

Open up the *PaddlesAppDelegate.m* file so you can import the new
TitleViewController class definition. Add the following to the existing import
statements:

```
#import "TitleViewController.h"
```

Modify the didFinishLaunchingWithOptions method to create a
TitleViewController and assign it to the **viewController** property. The
method should be modified to appear as follows:

```
- (BOOL)application:(UIApplication *)application
    didFinishLaunchingWithOptions:(NSDictionary *)launchOptions
{
    self.window = [[[UIWindow alloc]
                    initWithFrame:[[UIScreen mainScreen] bounds]]
                    autorelease];
    // Override point for customization after application launch.
    self.viewController = [[[TitleViewController alloc]
                            initWithNibName:@"TitleViewController"
                            bundle:nil] autorelease];
    self.window.rootViewController = self.viewController;
    [self.window makeKeyAndVisible];
    return YES;
}
```

The application delegate will now instantiate a **TitleViewController** not
the **PaddlesViewController**. But before you can run the application, you
need to modify the application delegate so that it does not call the pause
and resume methods on the **viewController**. This would cause a crash
since the **viewController** is now a **TitleViewController** and not a
PaddlesViewController. Modify the following application delegate methods
so the pause and resume calls are commented out:

```
- (void)applicationWillResignActive:(UIApplication *)application
{
    //[self.viewController pause];
}

- (void)applicationDidBecomeActive:(UIApplication *)application
```

```
{
    //[self.viewController resume];
}
```

Build and run the application. You should notice that the title view controller is displayed. Tap on each button to make sure the background of the button is toggled between the normal and hot image, as shown in Figure 6-5.

Figure 6-5. Button selected

The button actions have not been implemented to do anything yet, so you will work on that next. You need to create a couple methods in the application delegate that will allow playing of the game, and another method to show the title screen once the game finishes. You also need to add a new property to the **PaddlesViewController** so you know if the computer is playing or not. Add the following computer property to the **PaddlesViewController** interface:

```
@property (assign) int computer;
```

Add the following synthesize statement at the top of the *PaddlesViewController.m* file:

```
@synthesize computer;
```

You also need to add a new property to the application delegate that will hold the **PaddlesViewController** object when the game is started. Open the *PaddlesAppDelegate.h* file and add the following property to the list of existing properties:

```
@property (strong, nonatomic) PaddlesViewController *gameController;
```

Add declarations for **showTitle** and **playGame** methods in the application delegate header:

```
- (void)showTitle;
- (void)playGame: (int) computer;
```

The **playGame** method will allocate a new **PaddlesViewController** object, pass along the computer parameter, and then present the view controller modally. This will display the game on top of the existing title view controller. You will implement the **showTitle** method by dismissing the modally presented game controller. Add the following code into the application delegate implementation file:

```
- (void)showTitle
{
    // dismiss the game controller
    if (self.gameController)
    {
        [self.viewController dismissModalViewControllerAnimated:
                                                          NO];

        self.gameController = nil;
    }
}
- (void)playGame: (int) computer
{
    // present the game over the title
    if (self.gameController == nil)
    {
        self.gameController = [[[PaddlesViewController alloc]
                    initWithNibName:@"PaddlesViewController"
```

```
                                        bundle:nil] autorelease];
        self.gameController.computer = computer;

        [self.viewController presentModalViewController:
                        self.gameController animated:NO];
    }
}
```

Now you need to make a call to play the game when the buttons are tapped in the title view controller. Open the *TitleViewController.m* file and add the following import statement so you can access the application delegate and the new methods that were added:

```
#import "PaddlesAppDelegate.h"
```

You need to modify the **onPlay** implementation to get the application delegate and call the **playGame** method with the computer property. The sender object that is passed into the **onPlay** method needs to be cast into a **UIButton** control so the **tag** property can be accessed. Remember, you set the Computer button to have a **tag** value of 1. You can simply pass along the tag variable of the button to the **playGame** method. Modify the contents of the **onPlay** method to be the following:

```
- (IBAction)onPlay:(id)sender
{
    PaddlesAppDelegate *app = (PaddlesAppDelegate*)
        [UIApplication sharedApplication].delegate;
    UIButton *button = (UIButton*) sender;
    [app playGame: button.tag];
}
```

Run the game; notice it allows going from the title screen into a new game. However, once the game finishes, it does not return to the title screen. Open the *PaddlesViewController.m* implementation file and import the application delegate so you have access to call its methods, specifically the **showTitle** method:

```
#import "PaddlesAppDelegate.h"
```

Modify the code so when the alert view is dismissed, it will call the application delegate **showTitle** method versus just creating a new game. Modify the **alertView:didDismissWithButtonIndex** method so it appears as follows:

```
- (void)alertView:(UIAlertView *)alertView
            didDismissWithButtonIndex:(NSInteger)buttonIndex
{
    // message dismissed so reset the game and start animation
    alert = nil;

    // check if we should go back to title
    if ([self gameOver])
    {
        PaddlesAppDelegate *app = (PaddlesAppDelegate*)
            [UIApplication sharedApplication].delegate;
        [app showTitle];
        return;
    }

    // reset round
    [self reset];

    // start animation
    [self start];
}
```

Play the game again and make sure that it returns to the title screen after the game finishes. Now you need to add back the previous pause/resume logic, but this time you need to make sure that the game is actually playing. Obviously, if the title screen is displayed, there is nothing to pause or resume:

```
- (void)applicationWillResignActive:(UIApplication *)application
{
    // pause the game if active
    if (self.gameController)
    {
        [self.gameController pause];
    }
}
```

```
- (void)applicationDidBecomeActive:(UIApplication *)application
{
    // resume the game if active
    if (self.gameController)
    {
        [self.gameController resume];
    }
}
```

Make sure the pause/resume logic works by testing the screen lock on both the title screen and game screen. You should notice that, when in the title view, the pause and resume logic is ignored, and when playing the game, the game will pause and resume correctly.

Now you have a new title screen and the buttons to specify whether you want to play the computer player. Those buttons pass the computer value to the application delegate, which then passes it into the paddle view controller by setting the `computer` property. This allows the `PaddlesViewController` to know if the computer should be controlling one of the paddles.

Computer Player

Now for the fun part: you get to design a computer player from scratch. I find this to be the most interesting part of building any game, because you get the opportunity to model human behavior. How do you make a computer appear human? Or maybe a better question to ask is how do you make the computer seem less robotic? You will start this journey exactly the way I approached the problem, and that is by first creating the most basic computer player possible.

Basics

The most basic of computer players would simply just move the paddle around. Nothing more than that. And because the Paddle object is already geared to animate incremental steps of movement, it won't be very difficult. In the `PaddlesViewController` implementation, add the following method above the `animate` method:

- (void) computerAI

```
{
    // move paddle1 to a random position within player1 box
    float x = gPlayerBox[0].origin.x + arc4random() %
              (int) gPlayerBox[0].size.width;
    float y = gPlayerBox[0].origin.y + arc4random() %
              (int) gPlayerBox[0].size.height;
    [paddle1 move: CGPointMake(x,y)];
}
```

The **computerAI** method will just pick a random spot within the player box to move the paddle. Add the following code to the top of the **animate** function, so that when the computer is playing, it will call the **computerAI** method:

```
// check for computer player
if (computer)
{
    [self computerAI];
}
```

Build and run, then select the Computer player button from the title screen. You should notice that the paddle is now controlled by the computer, and it appears to be moving it in a berserk fashion. This is because the paddle is assigned a new position every frame of animation. This causes the paddle to shake very quickly because the code does not allow the paddle to arrive at its destination before a new random position is assigned. A quick fix to this is to monitor the speed of the paddle, and only assign a new position if the paddle is not moving. Modify the **computerAI** method to wait until the active speed of **paddle1** has been reduced to 0:

```
- (void) computerAI
{
    if (paddle1.speed == 0)
    {
        // move paddle1 to a random position within player1 box
        float x = gPlayerBox[0].origin.x + arc4random() %
                  (int) gPlayerBox[0].size.width;
        float y = gPlayerBox[0].origin.y + arc4random() %
                  (int) gPlayerBox[0].size.height;
        [paddle1 move: CGPointMake(x,y)];
```

```
        }
    }
```

Now the movements of the computer paddle has been downgraded from berserker to just a little crazy. At least the paddle now makes it to its destination before picking another position. There is one small issue you might have noticed, and that is you can still control the computer player's paddle by touching the top half of the screen. It's not very fair to be allowed to interfere with the computer's paddle. You should only allow control over the top paddle when the computer is not playing (**computer == 0**). Since the movement logic requires that a touch be assigned to a paddle, you only need to focus on the **touchesBegan** method. Modify the **touchesBegan** method to the following:

```
- (void)touchesBegan:(NSSet *)touches withEvent:(UIEvent *)event
{
    // iterate through our touch elements
    for (UITouch *touch in touches)
    {
        // get the point of touch within the view
        CGPoint touchPoint = [touch locationInView: self.view];

        // if paddle not already assigned a specific touch then
        // determine which half of the screen the touch is on
        // and assign it to that specific paddle
        if (paddle1.touch == nil && touchPoint.y < 240 &&
computer == 0)
        {
            touchPoint.y += 48;
            paddle1.touch = touch;
            [paddle1 move: touchPoint];
        }
        else if (paddle2.touch == nil)
        {
            touchPoint.y -= 32;
            paddle2.touch = touch;
            [paddle2 move: touchPoint];
        }
    }
}
```

You have just created an extremely simple—but very dumb—computer player. I want to take a step back in the next section and think about how to make a better computer player.

Human Model

Think about how you play the game of air hockey and all of the different decisions and behaviors you will typically make. The easiest state to understand is that of defense. You do not want the other player to score a point against you, so you will position the paddle in a way that makes it more difficult for the opponent to score. The next obvious state is offense, where you have the puck on your side of the table and it is under your control. At this point you will try and hit a powerful shot and hopefully score a point. I'll dive into these states in a bit, but for now I want you to think about a couple other states that might not be so obvious.

What about when the opponent has the puck and they aren't really doing anything? The opponent could be analyzing the board for the best shot possible. Maybe they will be creative and put together an angle shot. Maybe they just want to try for the best direct shot. What do you usually do when someone is holding on to the puck? Just sit still and let them prepare their shot? Not usually. You will move your paddle around into different positions so preparing for a good shot becomes more difficult. You want them to just take the shot, and not spend a lot of time preparing. Or maybe you are just bored and wished they would hurry up. Either way, you'll probably move your paddle around on the table. You already have the code that randomly moves the paddle around, so this will become the logic used in the bored state, as shown in Figure 6-6.

You also don't start in an offense, defense, or bored state, but usually in a state that makes a decision. Where is the puck? Should you go into defense or offense? Do you just wait and see what the other player does? The board needs to be analyzed and a decision on what to do next needs to be made. And maybe you will just decide to wait a little longer before a real decision is made. This will be the state that the computer will always fall back on after going into one of the other states. This will be the wait state for the computer. It will wait a random amount of time and then make an informed decision about what state it will go into next.

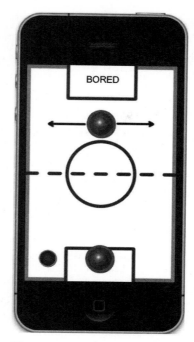

Figure 6-6. Bored State

Define all the different states the computer can be in by adding an enumeration into the **PaddlesViewController** header. Add the following line of code after the import statements and before the interface definition:

```
enum { AI_WAIT, AI_BORED, AI_DEFENSE, AI_OFFENSE };
```

Add a state variable inside the interface definition that will keep track of the active state the computer player is in. This will initially be set to 0, which is the **AI_WAIT** state:

```
int state;
```

At the start of every round, you need to reset the computer state back into the wait state. Add the following code into the **reset** method:

```
    // reset computer AI
    state = 0;
```

You will now create a basic implementation of the computer wait state. The first thing you will check is if the paddle is moving. Once the paddle comes to rest, the computer will start picking random numbers. Once the computer finds a specific number it will take action. This is basically how you will make the computer wait. It will just keep picking numbers until it gets the right one. Once it has picked the winning number, the computer will then be allowed to make a decision. It doesn't really matter what number it picks just as long as it is a specific one in the total range of random numbers. I decided to check if the random value picked was the number 1, and if so, the computer will decide on a new state to go into. For now, you will just have the computer enter into the bored state, but later on you will expand it to all the different states. Add the following to the top of the **computerAI** method:

```
if (state == AI_WAIT)
{
    // wait until paddle has stopped
    if (paddle1.speed == 0)
    {
        // pick a random number between 0 and 9
        int r = arc4random() % 10;

        // if we pick the number 1 then we go into a new state
        if (r == 1)
        {
            state = AI_BORED;
        }
    }
}
```

Why do you have the computer picking random numbers? The computer can obviously make quicker decisions than a human can, so you are making the computer player waste a few cycles before it makes a decision on which state it should go into. It also adds a bit of unpredictability to when the computer will enter a new state. Adding unpredictability to computer logic is always good, as it makes it more challenging for the player to figure out what the computer will do next.

Take the existing code that moves the paddle into a random position and make that the implementation of the bored state. The code after the wait state logic should be altered as follows:

```
// computer is bored and moves to random position
else if (state == AI_BORED)
{
    if (paddle1.speed == 0)
    {
        // move paddle into a random position within the
        // player1 box
        float x = gPlayerBox[0].origin.x + arc4random() %
                          (int) gPlayerBox[0].size.width;
        float y = gPlayerBox[0].origin.y + arc4random() %
                          (int) gPlayerBox[0].size.height;
        [paddle1 move: CGPointMake(x,y)];
        state = AI_WAIT;
    }
}
```

Now you should think about how the defensive state should be implemented.

Defense

I already discussed that the defensive state should make it difficult for the other player to score. But when does the computer take on a defensive position? Most likely when the other player has control of the puck, and definitely when the puck has been struck and is moving towards the top half of the table. What do you usually do when you are playing defensive? A good defense position, just like in soccer, is to put your paddle between the goal and the puck, as depicted in Figure 6-7. This prevents a straight-on shot making it difficult to get an easy point. It is also smart to pull the paddle back a little toward the goal to reduce chances of an angled shot, sneaking by the paddle. Pulling the paddle backwards can also help cushion the puck if it hits the paddle, which will hopefully keep it on the side of the table so you can then go into an offensive strategy. This logic will be the **AI_DEFENSE** state for the computer player.

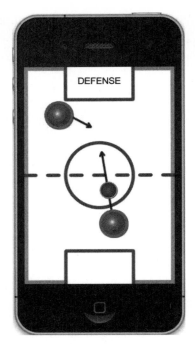

Figure 6-7. Moving to a good
defensive position

You will modify the **AI_WAIT** state to check if the puck is moving towards the top
of the screen, and if so it will go into the **AI_DEFENSE** state. In the defensive state,
you will initially create unbeatable logic by placing the paddle between the goal
and the incoming puck. You will move the paddle along the y-axis to the halfway
point between the goal and the puck. You will also position the paddle in the
same x-axis position as the puck. Once the puck speed has slowed down enough,
the computer will go back to the **AI_WAIT** state.

```
if (state == AI_WAIT)
{
    // wait until paddle has stopped
    if (paddle1.speed == 0)
    {
        // pick a random number between 0 and 9
        int r = arc4random() % 10;
```

```
        // if we pick the number 1 then we go into a
        // new state
        if (r == 1)
        {
            // if puck is heading towards us at a good rate
            // then go into defense
            if (puck.speed >= 1 && puck.dy < 0)
            {
                state = AI_DEFENSE;
            }
            else
            {
                state = AI_BORED;
            }
        }
    }
}
else if (state == AI_DEFENSE)
{
    // move to the puck x position and split the difference
    // between the goal
    [paddle1 move: CGPointMake(puck.center.x,
                               puck.center.y / 2) ];

    if (puck.speed < 1)
    {
        state = AI_WAIT;
    }
}
// computer is bored and moves to random position
else if (state == AI_BORED) ...
```

Go ahead and play the game at this point, and you should notice that the computer moves the paddle directly behind the puck when it goes into a defensive state. This looks a little bit robotic, in that the paddle is placed at the exact same location along the x-axis as the puck. I also noticed that sometimes the paddle stays in defensive position too long, especially when the puck has bounced off the paddle and is heading back towards the other goal. Let's modify the code so that it positions the paddle at an offset towards the center of the goal and also leaves the defensive state once the puck is heading back the other direction. I decided to offset the paddle toward the goal center by as much as the puck's width. This will help make the computer player look a little more natural. Modify the defensive implementation to the following:

```
// move to the puck x position and split the difference
// between the goal
float offset = ((puck.center.x - 160.0) / 160.0) * 40.0;
[paddle1 move: CGPointMake(puck.center.x - offset,
                           puck.center.y / 2) ];

if (puck.speed < 1 || puck.dy > 0)
{
    state = AI_WAIT;
}
```

The defensive strategy might be a little too good, as there really is no way to score if the computer is in that state. The only chance you can score is if it takes it a really long time to make a decision or it just went into a bored state, giving you a little time to make a shot. The game wouldn't be fun if you couldn't sneak a point even when the computer was playing defense, and one solution is to tweak the maximum speed that the paddle can move while in this state. This will allow you to shoot the puck by the computer player even if it is playing solid defense. Add the following line into the **AI_DEFENSE** logic:

paddle1.maxSpeed = MAX_SPEED / 3;

You need to reset the maximum speed back to the default once you go back into the wait state and the paddle has stopped moving. Add the following to the **AI_ WAIT** logic, right before the picking of the random number:

paddle1.maxSpeed = MAX_SPEED;

At this point the **computerAI** method should appear as follows:

```
- (void) computerAI
{
    if (state == AI_WAIT)
    {
        // wait until paddle has stopped
        if (paddle1.speed == 0)
```

```objc
    {
        paddle1.maxSpeed = MAX_SPEED;

        // pick a random number between 0 and 9
        int r = arc4random() % 10;

        // if we pick the number 1 then we go into a
        // new state
        if (r == 1)
        {
            // if puck is heading towards us at a good rate
            // then go into defense
            if (puck.speed >= 1 && puck.dy < 0)
            {
                state = AI_DEFENSE;
            }
            else
            {
                state = AI_BORED;
            }
        }
    }
}
else if (state == AI_DEFENSE)
{
    // move to the puck x position and split the difference
    // between the goal
    float offset = ((puck.center.x - 160.0) / 160.0) * 40.0;
    [paddle1 move: CGPointMake(puck.center.x - offset,
                                     puck.center.y / 2) ];

    if (puck.speed < 1 || puck.dy > 0)
    {
        state = AI_WAIT;
    }
    paddle1.maxSpeed = MAX_SPEED / 3;
}
// computer is bored and moves to random position
else if (state == AI_BORED)
{
```

```
    if (paddle1.speed == 0)
    {
        // move paddle into a random position within the
        // player1 box
        float x = gPlayerBox[0].origin.x + arc4random() %
                            (int) gPlayerBox[0].size.width;
        float y = gPlayerBox[0].origin.y + arc4random() %
                            (int) gPlayerBox[0].size.height;
        [paddle1 move: CGPointMake(x,y)];
        state = AI_WAIT;
    }
  }
}
```

Play the game with the new defensive state and you will notice it plays a much better game of air hockey. It is now much harder to score against the computer player. Even though the defense and bored states actually make for a better computer player, there still seems to be something missing. The computer rarely takes a shot unless it goes into the bored state and picks a random position on the board that collides with the puck. An offensive state needs to be added so the computer will go for the puck and take the shot when the time is right.

Offense

What makes for a good offensive strategy? Maybe you try and find a good angle shot that has a decent chance of getting in. Or maybe you just hit it as hard as possible not allowing for the opponent to prepare for the shot. When do you take the shot? Usually when you have control of the puck, which means, you wait until the puck has slowed down where you can hit it with a little more accuracy. So the computer should wait until the puck is on its side and not moving very fast before it takes a shot. This will be the AI_OFFENSE state for the computer player.

That part of the strategy seems obvious, but then I started thinking about how the computer should hit the puck. I pulled out a piece of paper and drew a few ideas down that might make for a good strategy. What if I calculated every angle that the paddle could hit the puck and simulate it out so the computer would know where the puck ended up. From there, I could rate the results such that if the puck scored a point it would rate that outcome higher than if a point wasn't scored. If the puck scored in your own goal then it could rate that very low. If you hit the back wall near the goal then that could be ranked higher than just hitting the player's paddle. I wanted to create a list of shots that were ranked by how good the shot resulted in. That would make for a pretty smart computer player, and then you could scale it back from there.

I started coding this strategy up for offense, and it is one of the reasons I created the *Puck* object, so it could be used to simulate out all the different possibilities. The *Puck* object can be modified so it can track the current puck position without using the view object. That way you could have multiple *Puck* objects that the computer used for simulation, and they wouldn't conflict with the current puck image on the screen. That wouldn't be a difficult modification and I initially went down this path to see what would happen. My first issue was how do I perform these calculations based on where the computer paddle is located. In order to get the proper angle, the paddle has to be moved into position first, and if the puck is moving then this information will get out of date quickly. I also assumed that if every single angle that the puck could be struck was simulated, that it might be too intense of a calculation and cause the game to lag. I needed a better solution that didn't require having to move the paddle into a specific angle to strike the puck and didn't require a lot of calculations.

My next idea was to pick a few random places that the paddle could hit the puck and then simulate that out to make a good decision. This would reduce the number of calculations, and also not require that the puck be put into a better position. You could just simulate it out from where the current puck and paddle were located. I decided this approach was much easier to implement and I started coding it up. The puck and paddle objects were modified so they could be simulated out without moving a view object. I ran a few tests and realized that the way the simulation was done, by calling the animate method per each frame, was just too slow to use for the computer simulations. You could tell when the computer ran its calculations the frame rates dropped. There was too much going on inside the animate method and it caused the game to lag. I needed an even simpler solution that didn't require a lot of processing power.

Sitting back in my chair, I decided my initial approach to offense was a horrible first approach. I spent a lot of time building this huge complicated system that required tons of calculations and processing power. Why would that be my step one? That's not how I typically code. I like to code in small increments so that I can see actual progress along the way. I think maybe I was just excited to come up with a really clever solution, rather than sticking to a simple approach that could be built upon.

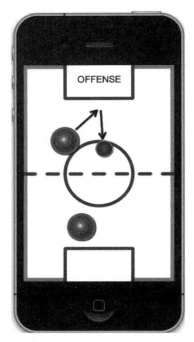

Figure 6-8. Offensive strategy

I painfully scrapped all my work and decided to think about using a simple solution. What is the absolute simplest method for an offensive strategy? Why not just hit the puck? That certainly would be the easiest approach possible to run with initially. All I needed to do was add to the decision logic so that if the puck is on the computer's side and the speed of the puck is slow enough, then it would change into the offensive state. The offense state would just move the paddle to the center position of the puck. It's simple: let's just hit the puck!

Modify the decision logic in the **AI_WAIT** state to include this logic for moving into the offense state:

```
        ...
                // if we pick the number 1 then we go into a
                // new state
                if (r == 1)
                {
                        // if puck is on our side and not moving fast
                        // go into offense. if puck is heading
                        // upwards with some speed go into defense.
                        // otherwise get bored

                        if (puck.center.y <= 240 && puck.speed < 1)
                        {
                            state = AI_OFFENSE;
                        }
                        else if (puck.speed >= 1 && puck.dy < 0)
                        {
                            state = AI_DEFENSE;
                        }
                        else
                        {
                            state = AI_BORED;
                        }
                }
        ...
```

Now you will add in the logic to just hit the puck when in the offense state. After you move the paddle to the puck's position, you will go back into the wait state. Add the following code to handle the **AI_OFFENSE** state:

```
    ...
    else if (state == AI_OFFENSE)
    {
        [paddle1 move: puck.center];
        state = AI_WAIT;
    }
    else if (state == AI_DEFENSE)
    ...
```

Now let's build and play the game and see how the offensive behavior of just hitting the puck works out. In my testing, I noticed that the computer will sometimes be in a defensive position, block the puck, wait until the puck slows, and then strike it. That was pretty cool to see, and it certainly appeared to have a human-like quality. On the other hand, when the puck gets behind the computer paddle, it will just blindly hit the puck in the wrong direction, sometimes sending the puck into the wrong goal. That's not a normal behavior and something you will fix a little later. Another problem that I noticed was sometimes the puck gets stuck in the corner for a little while, and the computer keeps trying to hit it but it doesn't move, so it hits it again, and so on. This results in the paddle just sitting on top of the puck and since the puck has nowhere to go, the paddle just keeps trying to hit it. If you haven't seen this condition occur, you can recreate it by simply placing the puck in the top left corner each round. Add the following code into the reset method to demonstrate the issue:

```
// test puck trap issue
viewPuck.center = CGPointZero;
```

Run the application again and you will see that sometimes the computer paddle gets trapped in the corner with the puck. This means the game would get stuck in a state where it could never finish, and that's not good. You need for the computer to move the paddle out of the way after it takes the shot. If you think about a human player, they will usually strike the puck, and pull back anyway. You could easily add the logic to move the paddle out of the way once it strikes it. Another way to solve the issue would be to test for the intersection of both the paddle and puck at the start of the **AI_WAIT** loop and then go into the **AI_BORED** state if that occurs. The objects usually won't be intersecting at the beginning of the **computerAI** method because the implementation of collision detection will reposition the objects so they are not overlapping. This doesn't always occur, however, because of the walls. So you could just check in this method if they are intersecting and then go into a bored state to correct. Another quick solution is instead of going into the **AI_WAIT** state from offense (which would result in going to offense again), you could set it to go directly into the **AI_BORED** state so the paddle moves to a random position. I decided to go with checking for intersection inside the **AI_WAIT** state, as it should offer the most protection against any type of trap condition. Add this to the top of the **AI_WAIT** logic:

```
if (state == AI_WAIT)
{
    // fix to handle computer trapping puck into the corner
    if ([paddle1 intersects: viewPuck.frame])
```

```
    {
        // go into a bored state so paddle moves to
        // random position
        state = AI_BORED;
        return;
    }
...
```

Test it again and you will notice that the computer paddle does in fact move away from the puck when it gets trapped. You may have noticed that this condition sometimes puts the computer paddle in position to score against itself. It might make sense to create a new state so when this trap condition occurs you can minimize the chances of this happening. I decided to focus on making the offensive behavior a little bit smarter than just going right for the puck. In the end, a smarter strike should help with the trap condition as well. Now that the trap problem has been solved, go ahead ahead and remove the debug code to place the puck in the top left corner.

Let's focus next on this issue where the computer blindly strikes the puck even if it is in front of it. In order to improve this, I want to make the offensive behavior have two parts to it. The first part will position the paddle in a striking position, and the second part will do the strike as it is coded now. Let's add a new state called **AI_OFFENSE2** to the **enum** definition at the top of the header file:

```
enum { AI_WAIT, AI_BORED, AI_DEFENSE, AI_OFFENSE, AI_OFFENSE2 };
```

The striking of the puck will be set to **AI_OFFENSE2**, and you will add a new **AI_OFFENSE** that moves the paddle into a random position behind the puck. This will help set up a better shot by making sure the paddle is behind the puck. Modify the offensive code to be handled in two parts as follows:

```
    else if (state == AI_OFFENSE)
    {
        // pick a new x position between -64 and +64
        // of puck center
        float x = puck.center.x - 64 + (arc4random() % 129);
        float y = puck.center.y - 64 - (arc4random() % 64);
        [paddle1 move: CGPointMake(x,y)];
        state = AI_OFFENSE2;
    }
```

```
    else if (state == AI_OFFENSE2)
    {
        if (paddle1.speed == 0)
        {
            // strike it
            [paddle1 move: puck.center];
            state = AI_WAIT;
        }
    }
```

Play the game and notice that the computer now sometimes hits an angled shot rather than just going straight for the puck. This makes it much more difficult to predict where the computer will take the shot. Another thing you may have noticed is the computer usually hits the puck before you do at the start of the round. This isn't very fair since you might have just dismissed the message dialog to start the game and may have not even have grabbed your paddle yet. It would be great if the computer would delay the first hit until you started moving your paddle, or at least wait a random amount of time before taking the initial shot. Let's add a new starting state that will handle this logic. Add the **AI_START** state to the beginning of the enumeration so that the computer player will always start in this state at the beginning of every round:

```
enum { AI_START, AI_WAIT, AI_BORED, AI_DEFENSE, AI_OFFENSE,
       AI_OFFENSE2 };
```

Now let's add starting logic that waits a random amount of time before going into the **AI_WAIT** state. It will also go into the **AI_WAIT** state if it notices the player's paddle has moved, which is reported when the player's paddle speed is greater than 0. Add the following logic to the top of the **computerAI** method before the **AI_WAIT** logic:

```
    if (state == AI_START)
    {
        if (paddle2.speed > 0 || (arc4random() % 100) == 1)
        {
            state = AI_WAIT;
        }
    }
    else if (state == AI_WAIT)
```

. . .

There are now 6 different computer states, which makes it difficult to know the active state the computer is currently in. You could modify each state handler and write a log message that tells you when the computer enters a new state. However, the states can change pretty quickly, making it difficult to keep an eye on both the computer's behavior and the current state. If you played it on device it would be even more difficult, as you can't really look at two different screens at the same time. In order to solve this, you will add a debug label to the top of the screen to display the active computer state.

Using interface builder, modify the *PaddlesViewController.xib* interface file and put a label at the top of the screen, as shown in Figure 6-9. Make sure the width is the size of the goal box, text color is black, and the alignment is centered. Create a property for the label and name it "debug." Now you will modify each state handler to update the label so the computer state is displayed on the screen. This will help validate all the current logic, and if you decide to add more states to the computer logic, it will help for that purpose, too.

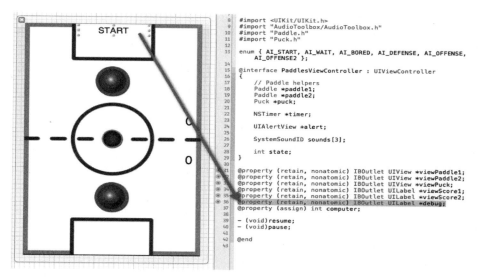

```objc
#import <UIKit/UIKit.h>
#import "AudioToolbox/AudioToolbox.h"
#import "Paddle.h"
#import "Puck.h"

enum { AI_START, AI_WAIT, AI_BORED, AI_DEFENSE, AI_OFFENSE,
       AI_OFFENSE2 };

@interface PaddlesViewController : UIViewController
{
    // Paddle helpers
    Paddle *paddle1;
    Paddle *paddle2;
    Puck *puck;

    NSTimer *timer;

    UIAlertView *alert;

    SystemSoundID sounds[3];

    int state;
}

@property (retain, nonatomic) IBOutlet UIView *viewPaddle1;
@property (retain, nonatomic) IBOutlet UIView *viewPaddle2;
@property (retain, nonatomic) IBOutlet UIView *viewPuck;
@property (retain, nonatomic) IBOutlet UILabel *viewScore1;
@property (retain, nonatomic) IBOutlet UILabel *viewScore2;
@property (retain, nonatomic) IBOutlet UILabel *debug;
@property (assign) int computer;

- (void)resume;
- (void)pause;

@end
```

Figure 6-9. Debug label

Here is the entire **computerAI** function with the debug label updated:

```objc
- (void) computerAI
{
    if (state == AI_START)
    {
        debug.text = @"START";

        if (paddle2.speed > 0 || (arc4random() % 100) == 1)
        {
            state = AI_WAIT;
        }
    }
    else if (state == AI_WAIT)
    {
        // fix to handle computer trapping puck into the corner
        if ([paddle1 intersects: viewPuck.frame])
        {
            // go into a bored state so paddle moves to
            // random position
            state = AI_BORED;
            return;
        }

        // wait until paddle has stopped
        if (paddle1.speed == 0)
        {
            debug.text = @"WAIT";

            paddle1.maxSpeed = MAX_SPEED;

            // pick a random number between 0 and 9
            int r = arc4random() % 10;

            // if we pick the number 1 then we go into a
            // new state
            if (r == 1)
            {
                // if puck is on our side and not moving fast
```

```
            // go into offense. if puck is heading
            // upwards with some speed go into defense.
            // otherwise get bored
            if (puck.center.y <= 240 && puck.speed < 1)
            {
                state = AI_OFFENSE;
            }
            else if (puck.speed >= 1 && puck.dy < 0)
            {
                state = AI_DEFENSE;
            }
            else
            {
                state = AI_BORED;
            }
        }
    }
}
else if (state == AI_OFFENSE)
{
    debug.text = @"OFFENSE";

    // pick a new x position between -64 and +64
    // of puck center
    float x = puck.center.x - 64 + (arc4random() % 129);
    float y = puck.center.y - 64 - (arc4random() % 64);
    [paddle1 move: CGPointMake(x,y)];
    state = AI_OFFENSE2;
}
else if (state == AI_OFFENSE2)
{
    debug.text = @"OFFENSE2";

    if (paddle1.speed == 0)
    {
        // strike it
        [paddle1 move: puck.center];
        state = AI_WAIT;
    }
}
```

```
else if (state == AI_DEFENSE)
{
    debug.text = @"DEFENSE";

    // move to the puck x position and split the difference
    // between the goal
    float offset = ((puck.center.x - 160.0) / 160.0) * 40.0;
    [paddle1 move: CGPointMake(puck.center.x - offset,
                                puck.center.y / 2) ];

    if (puck.speed < 1 || puck.dy > 0)
    {
        state = AI_WAIT;
    }
    paddle1.maxSpeed = MAX_SPEED / 3;
}
// computer is bored and moves to random position
else if (state == AI_BORED)
{
    if (paddle1.speed == 0)
    {
        debug.text = @"BORED";

        // move paddle into a random position within the
        // player1 box
        float x = gPlayerBox[0].origin.x + arc4random() %
                        (int) gPlayerBox[0].size.width;
        float y = gPlayerBox[0].origin.y + arc4random() %
                        (int) gPlayerBox[0].size.height;
        [paddle1 move: CGPointMake(x,y)];
        state = AI_WAIT;
    }
}
}
```

In the next section, you will add different levels of difficulty to the computer player.

Computer Difficulty

You will now create easy, medium, and hard difficulty levels for the computer player. The way I like to approach the computer difficulty is to adjust the characteristics of the existing logic to make it easier or harder. A lot of times, you can just tweak the numbers behind the logic itself. It also helps to have the difficulty setting as a numeric value, such as an integer, so you can use it directly in the equations for computer behavior. You probably remember that the computer property is currently an integer and not just a Boolean or string value. The reason was so you could easily add support for difficulty without having to change much, especially within the interface itself.

The title view currently has two buttons to pick between computer or two-player mode. You are using the same method to handle both selections, with the only difference being that the Tag variable of the button is 0 for two players and 1 for computer. You can just set computer difficulty using the same method by changing the computer player button to be three buttons. Each computer button will have an incrementing Tag value for difficulty. You will assign a Tag value of 1 for easy, 2 for medium, and 3 for hard. The great thing about this is you can use the exact same **onPlay** handler. The value of the tag property is simply passed along to the application delegate, and then to the **PaddlesViewController**, so no extra coding will be required.

Open up the *PaddlesViewController.xib* file and copy and paste the Computer button twice. Rename the Computer button labels to say "Easy," "Medium," and "Hard," and lay them out as shown in Figure 6-10. Using the Attributes Inspector, set the Tag property for the Easy button to 1, Medium button to 2, and Hard button to 3. And that is all you have to do, as the action outlet was copied to the new buttons. How simple was that?

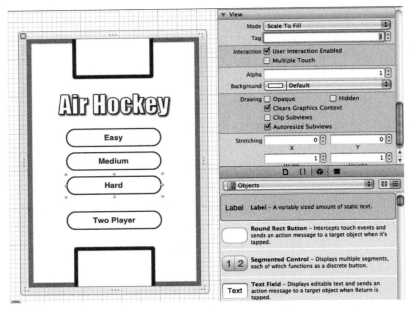

Figure 6-10. Computer difficulty-level buttons

All of the buttons should continue to work with the computer difficulty buttons just playing against the current computer logic. The only difference is now the computer property represents more than just that the computer is playing, it also includes how difficult the computer player should be. You can probably think of a few things that you can do to scale the difficulty of the computer, such as slowing the paddle down or delaying how long it takes the computer to make a decision. You will use those techniques and a few others to give a different playing experience for each level picked. I will now tackle each computer state, one at a time, and tweak it to use the computer property to scale difficulty.

Look at the **AI_START** state and see what could be adjusted for computer difficulty. It makes sense to have the harder computer player come out of the starting state faster than the easy player. It currently picks a random number to decide when to move into the **AI_WAIT** state, so you could reduce the total amount of numbers that it picks from to speed things up on average. Modify the start condition to be as follows:

```
if (state == AI_START)
```

```
    {
        debug.text = @"START";

        if (paddle2.speed > 0 ||
            (arc4random() % (100/computer)) == 1)
        {
            state = AI_WAIT;
        }
    }
```

Notice that all I'm doing is dividing the available pool of random numbers by the computer property. No need to worry about division by zero (which would crash the program) since **computer** will always be 1 or greater in this method. Now when you are playing easy mode, it will use 100 as the value, medium will use 50, and hard will use 33. You can hopefully see why it's nice to keep difficulty as a numeric value, so you can very easily integrate the value within the computer logic. You could easily have had a whole series of conditional statements checking if you were playing easy, medium, or hard, and then providing completely different logic for each one. But hopefully you will agree that this is a much simpler approach and ultimately leads to less code. And less code means fewer bugs.

Let's look at the **AI_WAIT** code now and see what can be adjusted. Just like you did for the start condition, you can adjust the total pool of random numbers to pick from so the computer will make quicker decisions when playing the harder levels. You are currently picking from a total of 10 numbers. If you divide that number by the computer level like you did before, that would result in 10, 5, and 3 for easy, medium, and hard, respectively. I decided to use 12, 8, and 4 instead, so that the medium and hard levels were not drastically more difficult. I also felt that the easy level could be a little slower at making decisions than the current computer behavior. Modify the range of random numbers to the following:

```
int r = arc4random() % ((4 - computer) *4);
```

The next part of code you want to modify is when to go into the offensive state. You probably have noticed when playing the game that it takes a while for the computer to strike the puck. This is because it waits until the puck is almost stopped. The computer player would be more difficult if you allowed it to take a shot when the puck was travelling at faster speeds. This would increase the speed at which the computer takes shots, which ultimately means the gameplay will be faster. You will modify the minimum puck speed requirement of 1 to be the computer level. This means that the puck speed will have to be less than 1 for easy, less than 2 for medium, and less than 3 for hard level. Another change you can make is when you are in easy mode, you could skip the **AI_OFFENSE** state, and go straight into **AI_OFFENSE2** so it takes the shot. This means easy mode will not reposition the paddle before taking the shot, so it will be more predictable and make more mistakes. The medium and hard levels will continue to reposition the paddle randomly behind the puck by going into the **AI_OFFENSE** state. Change the offensive decision code to the following:

```
...
        if (puck.center.y <= 240 && puck.speed < computer)
        {
            if (computer == 1) state = AI_OFFENSE2;
                else state = AI_OFFENSE;
        }
...
```

Let's take a look at the **AI_OFFENSE** state and see what can be modified. This state positions the paddle randomly behind the puck before it strikes. You just modified the code so that only medium and hard levels use this state. When not playing the hard level, let's slow down the paddle movement to half of the max speed. Modify the offense-state code as follows:

```
...
    else if (state == AI_OFFENSE)
    {
        debug.text = @"OFFENSE";

        if (computer < 3) paddle1.maxSpeed = MAX_SPEED / 2;

        // pick a new x position between -64 and +64
        // of puck center
        float x = puck.center.x - 64 + (arc4random() % 129);
        float y = puck.center.y - 64 - (arc4random() % 64);
        [paddle1 move: CGPointMake(x,y)];
        state = AI_OFFENSE2;
    }
```

. . .

The **AI_OFFENSE2** state strikes the puck at maximum speed. Modify it so that only the hard level hits the puck at max speed. You will set the easy level to only strike at 1/2 the max speed and change medium level to strike at 3/4 of max speed. Modify the code as follows:

. . .

```
    else if (state == AI_OFFENSE2)
    {
        debug.text = @"OFFENSE2";
        if (computer == 1)
        {
            paddle1.maxSpeed = MAX_SPEED / 2;
        }
        else if (computer == 2)
        {
            paddle1.maxSpeed = MAX_SPEED * 3/4;
        }
        // strike it
        [paddle1 move: puck.center];
        state = AI_WAIT;
    }
```

. . .

The **AI_DEFENSE** state positions the paddle between the goal box and the puck. Modify the code so that it moves the paddle into position faster for the medium and hard levels. You will keep the easy level at 1/3 of maximum speed, and then adjust medium to 2/5 and hard to 1/2 of max speed.

. . .

```
    else if (state == AI_DEFENSE)
    {
        debug.text = @"DEFENSE";
        // move to the puck x position and split the difference
        // between the goal
        float offset = ((puck.center.x - 160.0) / 160.0) * 40.0;
        [paddle1 move: CGPointMake(puck.center.x - offset,
                                    puck.center.y / 2) ];
        if (puck.speed < 1 || puck.dy > 0)
        {
```

```
            state = AI_WAIT;
        }
    if (computer == 1)
    {
        paddle1.maxSpeed = MAX_SPEED / 3;
    }
    else if (computer == 2)
    {
        paddle1.maxSpeed = MAX_SPEED * 2/5;
    }
    else if (computer == 3)
    {
        paddle1.maxSpeed = MAX_SPEED / 2;
    }
}
```

...

The **AI_BORED** state picks a random position within the player box and moves the puck into it. You can change the paddle speed to make it take longer to move to the random position, which of course makes it easier to allow the player to sneak a shot into the goal. You can also make the rectangle that is used to pick that random position to be smaller and closer to the goal box. This will make the position selected more defensive and more difficult to score against. Modify the handling of the bored state to be as follows:

```
else if (state == AI_BORED)
{
    if (paddle1.speed == 0)
    {
        debug.text = @"BORED";

        // change paddle speed based on level
        paddle1.maxSpeed = 3 + computer;

        // inset the rectangle if medium (20) or hard (40)
        int inset = (computer - 1) * 20;

        // move paddle into a random position within the
        // player1 box
```

```
        float x = (gPlayerBox[0].origin.x + inset) +
                  arc4random() %
                  (int) (gPlayerBox[0].size.width - inset*2);
        float y = gPlayerBox[0].origin.y +
                  arc4random() %
                  (int) (gPlayerBox[0].size.height - inset);

        [paddle1 move: CGPointMake(x,y)];
        state = AI_WAIT;
    }
}
```

You now have three different computer players each with different characteristics. Play the game on each level and take notice of the current computer state and the movements that the computer player makes. Hopefully you will find that it is easier to win on the easy level, and that the hard level gives you a pretty good challenge. If that is not the case then you can always go back and make adjustments to the numbers. There is no right answer but I encourage you to let others determine if the game is difficult or not. As the developer, you know the code behind the game, so it can be difficult to judge if things are easy or not. Always let others play the game and get as much feedback as possible before launching it in the App Store. Chances are your friends will bring up the same concerns as others who download your game. It is best to come out of the gate with the best product possible.

Once you are satisfied with the computer logic, you should take out the debug message at the top of the screen. You could remove it completely, although you may want to use it again in the future, so let's just make it invisible instead. If you ever want to add more computer states or even adjust the current implementation, using the debug message can be an invaluable tool. In order to make the message invisible, add the following to the **viewDidLoad** method:

```
debug.hidden = YES;
```

You now have a completed iPhone game that supports both two-player and computer modes. The computer mode supports multiple difficulty levels that you can progress through. All that is left is submitting it for review and hopefully getting it approved for distribution in the App Store. I'll cover that in the next chapter.

7

App Store

I will walk you through the process of submitting your application to the App Store. There have been numerous improvements to the iTunes Connect website since it was first introduced. The process has gotten a lot easier to submit an application, and now there are many automated checks that validate your submission immediately. The longest part of this entire process, outside of waiting for your application to get reviewed, is creating all the screenshots and coming up with a description of your application. Once that has been done, the actual submit process is very simple and won't take long. I will also discuss things you can do after your application has been approved that will help drive more downloads. Before we get to that, I will walk you through submitting your first application.

Screenshots

I want you to take a few compelling screenshots of your application. You could do this using the iPhone Simulator on the Mac, but I find the easiest method is to use the device itself. Screenshots can be taken on the device by holding down the screen lock button and pressing the home button at the same time. You will see the iPhone screen flash and a photo of whatever was on the screen will be dropped into your Camera Roll. I suggest taking a lot of different screenshots, making sure to show the unique parts of your game. The first screenshot is the most important; it should be a good action shot from the game. My first screenshot, shown in Figure 7-1, is of a game in progress with an active score. You can then add other screenshots, such as the title screen, which would show all the different options of play for the air hockey game. Anything that looks good and will help the customer make a buy decision.

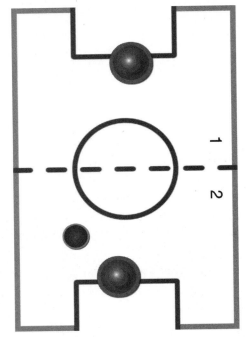

Figure 7-1. Air hockey screenshot

If you use the Simulator to take a screenshot, you can use the keyboard shortcut Command-Shift-4, press the space bar, and then click on the Simulator window. This will grab the entire contents of the Simulator, including the iPhone graphic, and save it as an image on the Desktop. This image will work great on your website but will need to be cropped to the actual device screen size for the App Store. Just use your favorite photo editor and crop out the Simulator screen contents to the correct dimensions mentioned below.

You are allowed to have five screenshots for each application, so try and take that many if possible. If you can't come up with enough unique types of screenshots it's okay; you don't need to use them all. It is a requirement to have at least one though. Remember, most people go right to the screenshots to decide if they will buy your game or not, so it is important to put your best shots first. The screenshots can be the standard resolution of 320×480 or the Retina display high resolution of 640×960. The screenshots can be in either portrait or landscape orientations. If your game supports Retina display it is best to use that format. I always use my iPod 4th generation or iPhone 4 to take the screenshots, so the resulting images will be high resolution. If you use an older device, you will be limiting yourself to the standard resolution.

Once you have taken all your screenshots, transfer them over to your Mac using software such as the free iPhoto. I usually create a new album with the same name as the game and import all the photos from the device there. I have recently been using the Dropbox iPhone app to quickly get the photos off the device and into a folder on my computer. Once all the photos have been grabbed off the device, go through each one, and decide the order that you want to publish them in. Try and tell a story with your screenshots, something that will grab your audience. Or you can just order them by the most impressive looking screenshots first. Sometimes it is good to put captions along with your screen shots, just to highlight key features of the game. Again, most people browse screenshots first to see if they are interested and then read the description.

I rename my photos prior to submitting so I know the exact order to upload them to iTunes Connect. For example, *AirHockey1–5.png* would tell me to submit *AirHockey1.png*, followed by *AirHockey2.png*, and so on. Try and keep everything organized, as you will most likely need these photos again.

Creating the Application Description and Keywords

Open up your favorite text editor or word processing application and create a new document. I usually use Microsoft Word, so I get the benefits of spelling and grammar checks against the application description and keywords. You could go straight to iTunes Connect and type this information in, but it usually takes a while to come up with something good and you don't want your web session timing out on you. You will probably also use the description and keywords on your own website, so it's good to keep a local copy.

The first thing you will need to decide is what is: the name of your game? The name has to be unique from all other apps in the App Store. The best thing to do is to first search the iTunes App Store and see if the name you want is already taken. You will also need to make sure that you name it something that is not trademarked by another company. You should also search Google for the name, as well as the United States Patent and Trademark Office (*www.uspto.gov*) website. You want your game to be unique so that people can easily find it. The application name is indexed when searching for apps within the iTunes App Store.

Now let's work on the application description, which is the text that a customer first reads when they pull up your application in iTunes. This field is not search indexed inside of iTunes, so this is merely a way to convey to the potential customer exactly what your game does and why they should buy it. The desktop version of iTunes displays the first 3 lines of the application description and collapses the rest. On the device, I typically only read the first paragraph and then scroll to the screenshots. This is why the first few sentences are very important. Try to grab the customers attention in the first sentence. I wrote this as my first paragraph for Air Hockey:

> Now you can carry the game of Air Hockey in your pocket! Includes realistic game play, intuitive multi-touch controls, and it's FREE. Play head-to-head with a friend or challenge the computer with multiple difficulty levels. Hear the puck smack against your paddle, watch it glide with realistic physics, and feel the excitement as the puck drops into your opponent's goal.

Keep the application description honest and only mention features that are currently supported in the game. It is important not to mention pricing information in the application description, as Apple will most likely not approve it. This is because pricing information is converted to the local currency of the iTunes user, so if you said "ONLY $0.99," then that wouldn't match what someone in the UK would see on the purchase button. It is okay to say "free" or "free for a limited time," which might help get more customers playing your game before charging a price for it.

The next data you will need are the keywords, which are extremely important. Keywords, along with application name, are used when someone searches iTunes. You should pick good keywords that will help users find your application. The App Store, when it first opened, used the application description for search matching, but this was quickly abused. People would throw in tons of keywords that didn't even match what the application did. Apple then made a change to not index the application description and required developers to supply keywords that were limited to 100 characters. This doesn't allow you to add a ton of keywords so you have to choose wisely. Each keyword is also separated by a comma and you don't need to include spaces. The commas also count towards the maximum character limit. You might find it useful to use a character counter so you can make sure you are using the most characters possible. There are many available online that allow you to paste in the keywords and get the total count. It is really important to submit as many keywords as iTunes Connect will allow.

A great resource for helping you find good keywords is Google AdWords (*https://adwords.google.com/*). Although this is the website that allows you to advertise within Google search results, it includes a keyword optimization tool that helps you find keywords people use when searching for certain terms. I find it to be an extremely useful tool for finding popular keywords and it doesn't cost you anything to use the tool. What are people searching for when they want to find "Air Hockey"? The Google keyword optimization tool can answer that.

Always spell check your work, as a poorly written description might make people think your game is also poorly written. Save the document in a location along with all your screenshots because you will most likely need all of this for your own website.

Submitting Metadata to iTunes Connect

Now that you have the screenshots, application description, and keywords, you can go ahead and submit that information to Apple. The iTunes Connect website (*https://iTunesConnect.apple.com/*) is where you submit all the information that iTunes needs to allow people to find your application. It also manages your contracts, tax, and billing information, which are required if you are charging money for your app. In addition, it provides sales information of your app once it is available for download in the App Store.

Log in to iTunes Connect and click Manage Your Applications. This is the screen that allows you to update existing applications and add new ones. Click the Add New App button to start the process of submitting the app information. This brings you to a screen that asks for the App Name, SKU Number, and Bundle ID. The App Name needs to be unique and cannot be longer than 255 bytes. You will be told if the name is not unique when you submit. I always do a few searches on iTunes to see if others have similar names. This doesn't always work though, as developers can sit on a name for up to 90 days before actually submitting it to the store.

Registering an application name before actually submitting the application is a good idea because it gives you time to promote the name of the application before it actually hits the store. Once the application name is registered then nobody else can register it for the next 90 days. Make sure you know the application can be submitted in this time frame, because if it is not then your time will expire and you will not be able to register that name again.

The SKU Number is a unique number that you have to assign to the application. Although it asks for a number, you can use letters as well, and I typically use the application name in all caps with underscores if necessary. For example, if I was submitting the application named "Air Hockey" I would use "AIR_HOCKEY" for the SKU number. This is the only piece of metadata that you cannot change later, as it is only used internally and on sales reports. The value is never displayed to the customer.

The Bundle ID is a drop-down box that allows you to select any App ID you created in the iOS Provisioning Portal. In my case, I had registered a wild card App ID of "com.toddmoore.*" that allows me to submit multiple apps with the same App ID. This does not allow for Apple Push Notification services or Game Center support, so if you need those features you will have to create a specific App ID for the application. Once you create the App ID it will be available in the drop-down box. Since I selected a wild card App ID, I have to add an additional Bundle ID suffix to make it unique. This needs to match the same bundle ID that was used when the Xcode project was created. In my case, I used "AirHockey" as the suffix, which sets the full Bundle ID to "com.toddmoore.AirHockey" ...and that matches what was used in the project.

Now that this information has been entered, click the Continue button and see if there are any issues. You will be presented with any errors that are discovered, such as "The App Name you entered has already been used." This error was presented to me when I attempted to use the name "Air Hockey," because somebody else had already taken the name. I tried a few variations, such as "Air Hockey Free," "Air Hockey Pro," and "Air Hockey Extreme," but they were all taken. I decided to add the name of this book to the end, making the application name "Air Hockey: Tap, Move, Shake"—which is probably a better title anyway because the app will be displayed if someone searches for this book in iTunes.

The next screen allows you to set the Availability Date and Price Tier. I usually set the availability date to be a month into the future. Once the application is approved, I will go in and modify it to the day I want it released. There was a time that having a date set to a date in the past would cause your application to be pushed further down in the Release Date list on iTunes. This made it more difficult to be found and you wouldn't get a nice first day spike from people finding your app in this list. It appears Apple has finally fixed the issue, so going with an older date shouldn't put you at a disadvantage, it will just release your application as soon as it is approved.

You can select a price for your application or make it free. In my case, I'm going to make this game free so anyone can play it and see if it is something they would like to learn how to build. If you want to charge money for your game, you need to select a Price Tier. These tiers currently range from $0.99 to $999.99 for the US market. Click on the Pricing Matrix link to see how each tier maps to a price and the proceeds you will receive, which works out to be 70% of the sale. I recommend sticking to a lower amount such as $0.99 or $1.99 for iPhone games. The App Store's Top Paid category is based on sales and not revenue, so if you ever want your application to reach the top charts, it usually has to be priced cheap so it can compete for a ranking. There is a Top Grossing category that is based on total revenue and shows who is making the most money in the App Store. This is an interesting category because it shows that developers are making money releasing free apps that contain in-app purchasing ability. It's always a good idea to visit the App Store and see which apps are making the most money. It might help you decide on what kind of game or app to build if you have a bunch of ideas. Click the Continue button to submit this information and go to the next screen.

The Version Number needs to be specified next. If you had already published your game somewhere else, for example in the Mac App Store, and it is based on the same source code or feature set then you will probably use the same version. If this is your first version, assigning it 1.0 is usually what I specify. You can always update your application down the road but you will have to increase the version number, such that it is higher than the previous. For example, if you submitted version 1.0, you could then submit an update called 1.1 or even 1.0.1.

When updating an application, it is useful to follow a format that conveys how major of an update it is. I use the format `MAJOR.MINOR.REVISION`, where the `MAJOR` digit is only increased when major functionality is added to the app. Increasing the `MINOR` digit implies new minor features have been added. An increase to the `REVISION` digit is done only to fix bugs with the current version. This is how I implement my version scheme and it has worked well for me, but you can choose to implement something different, as long as one of the numbered digits has increased in value. If you change multiple digits then the highest digit changed needs to be increased. For example, you can submit a 3.1.2 upgrade to version 3.0.5 since the second digit increased from 0 to 1. You could also go from version 3.1.2 to 4.0, which would imply a major upgrade from version 3 to 4.

Let's take a simple example where you submitted version 1.0 of Air Hockey with only two-player support. The next release added a computer player, which is a big enough feature that would be worthy of a 2.0 release. You then followed that version with different computer difficulty levels and called it a 2.1 release. After publishing that version, you realized you had a small bug that needed fixing. You then submitted a 2.1.1 release to address the glitch, which is appropriate because this version only fixes bugs and doesn't add any additional features.

Now fill in the rest of the following metadata:

- Description: Just paste in the application description that you already typed up. This is not a rich text editor, so the text cannot be formatted using different fonts or styles such as bold and italics. Just make sure the text you pasted into the field maintains the hard returns after each paragraph.

- Primary Category: Select Games and pick two subcategories. I selected "Sports" and "Family" for this game but you can pick anything you want.

- Secondary Category: This category is only used for when people are searching iTunes within a specific category. I selected "Entertainment" as my secondary category. The application will not be listed in this category and is only viewable if people are searching (not browsing) the category. The primary category is much more important.

- Keywords: Paste in the keywords you already selected in the previous section. It is limited to 100 bytes so you might get an error if you exceed this amount. If so, you will need to start deleting keywords that are less important until you are below the limit.

- Copyright: I set my copyright for Paddles and Air Hockey to be "2011 Todd Moore." If you have registered as a company, then you would want to use the name of that entity.

- Contact Email Address: It is best to set up a different email address than your personal email. I used *support@toddmoore.com* for this purpose. This email address will be listed on a lot of websites, so it will receive a lot of spam.

- Support URL: This should be your website. I used *http://toddmoore.com/* and that is where people can get in touch with me.

- App URL: This is optional but it is a really good idea to include it. Many websites scrape the iTunes listings and publish all the links on their site. This will help improve your website ranking within search engines. I used *http://toddmoore.com/book/* as my URL.

- Review Notes: You can pass along any messages to the person who is reviewing your application at Apple. If your app requires an account login, you need to pass along demo credentials so the reviewer can login. You can also pass along tips or cool things that the reviewer should check out. If you put in an easter egg into your game, you will need to let the reviewer know how to access it.

- Rating: I selected None all the way down, which gives an age ranking of 4. This is what decides if devices with age restrictions set by parents can download your app. Apple reserves the right to tweak these values.

- EULA: If you need to create your own End User License Agreement, you can add that to this section. If you do not provide one then the standard EULA gets applied to your application. I am not submitting a custom EULA and have always used the standard EULA provided by Apple. If you are including libraries that require separate licensing then you can add that here.

- Uploads: Click the Choose File button for the Application Icon and select the large 512×512 icon that was created in Chapter 3, the graphics chapter. Now add all the screenshots you created in the previous section under the iPhone and iPod touch Screenshots. You are not submitting a universal app but if you were then you would also have to attach iPad Screenshots.

Click the Save button and your application metadata is now saved in draft form. You can always pull this information back up and edit it before you submit the application , as shown in Figure 7-2. The application will now be in a new state called "Prepare for Upload," which is what you will do next. If you are going to submit your application later, then you are done. When you are ready to submit, you will have to open the application information page up again, click View Details for the current version, and then press the Ready to Upload Binary button. This puts the application entry into a "Waiting for Upload" state, which allows the app to be archived and submitted for review.

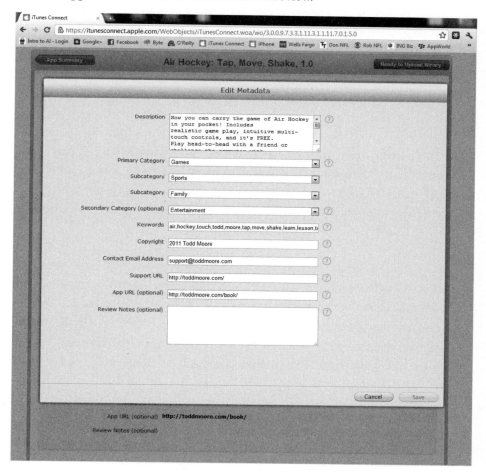

Figure 7-2. Editing app metadata

Archive and Submit

Archiving the application allows you to submit it to iTunes Connect or share with others. The process builds the application in release mode, which results in faster code. Up until this point you have been running the application built for debugging. The final version of your application will not include debug symbols and it will be optimized, making it faster. When the compiler optimizes code, it creates a completely different binary that can result in different application behaviors. For this reason it is extremely important that you always test out the release build of your application on a device before submitting to the App Store.

> In order to build in release mode you will need to edit your current scheme. Select Product→Edit Scheme and for the Run action change the build configuration from Debug to Release. If you build with that configuration, it will result in running the app with the same configuration used for submitting to the App Store. Make sure to test all aspects of your application to ensure all features work as they did in debug mode.

Once you have completed testing, select Product→Archive to build and zip the application so you can submit to the App Store. This will bring up Organizer, which allows you to access all the archives you have created per application. You can always access the Organizer by selecting Window→Organizer from Xcode. Once the archive has been built and selected inside the Organizer, you have the option to validate or submit to the iTunes Connect website, as shown in Figure 7-3.

You should validate the application first so that iTunes Connect can run a series of automated tests against the application binary. You will be prompted to enter your iTunes Connect credentials, followed by the appropriate signing identity, which will be the same App Store certificate you used to sign the target. This doesn't mean your application will be approved or accepted, but it at least lets you know the application is not missing anything important like a properly sized icon. If it fails validation, you will receive an error and a description of how to fix it. If you need more information, you can always Google the error returned and usually you'll find other developers who had the same problem and a solution for how to fix it.

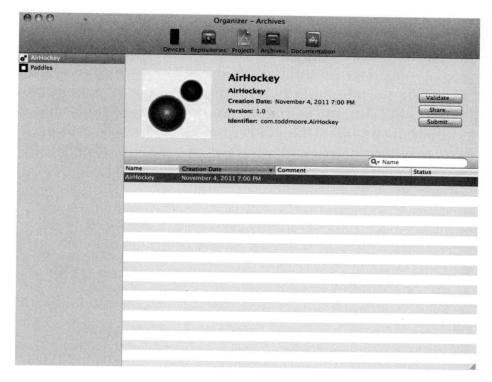

Figure 7-3. Xcode organizer

Now that your application has passed validation, it is time to submit to iTunes Connect. Just follow the same procedure you used for validating the application but this time choose Submit versus Validate to kick off the process. Enter all the same information, including the iTunes Connect credentials and your App Store certificate. Once the submission has been uploaded, you will be notified if the binary has been rejected or is waiting for approval.

If your binary is rejected, you will have to resubmit and fix whatever errors were reported. The most common reason rejection occurs is not using the correct certificate for App Store distribution. If this happens to you go back into your project and make sure the project target build options have the correct App Store signing certificate specified for release mode.

App Review

The application review involves an engineer at Apple reviewing your application on an iOS device. I have lost count how many times a new application or application update was rejected. I think I've been rejected for about every reason on their checklist. So don't feel bad if your first attempt ends in failure because there is a lot to know. The good news is games are usually a lot easier to get through the review process, as you have creative freedom when it comes to your interface. If you're building an application based on the standard UI controls, such as table views, navigation controllers, and stock buttons, then your app will be reviewed so it meets Apple's Human Interface Guidelines. This document can be accessed within the Xcode documentation and on the Apple developer website. I highly recommend reading it over, especially if you are creating regular applications.

The most common reason they deny applications, according to Apple, is because the app fails to launch. There are many reasons for why your application could crash right at startup during the application initialization process. Maybe you are using a feature that isn't available on the hardware or iOS version they are using. Maybe your application does too many object allocations at startup, which consumes too much memory and the app gets killed. One test they always run is making sure your application starts up in Airplane Mode. If your application requires an Internet connection, you have to make sure those functions do not crash the application when the Internet is unavailable.

I have compiled a few of my own rejections, which should help prepare you for the worst.

> Dear Developer,
>
> Your application, Card Counter, cannot be posted to the App Store at this time because it does not adhere to the iPhone Human Interface Guidelines as outlined in iPhone SDK Agreement section 3.3.5.
>
> When the device is not connected to network, attempting to 'Submit high score' does not give a transmission error and score disappears from the scoreboard. This behavior might lead to user

confusion. It would be appropriate to display either a notification or an alert stating that Internet connectivity is required.

Please review the Handling Common Tasks section of the iPhone's Human Interface Guidelines here: *https://developer.apple .com/iphone/library/documentation/UserExperience/Conceptual/ MobileHIG*

In order for your application to be reconsidered for the App Store, please resolve this issue and upload your new binary to iTunes Connect. Should you require more assistance with resolving this issue, Apple Developer Technical Support is available to provide direct one-on-one support for discrete code-level questions.

Regards,

iPhone Developer Program

Always make sure when submitting data over the network that you display a notification to the user if it fails. At a minimum you could display this error condition with a simple alert dialog. Just remember to always check this condition by putting your device in Airplane Mode and testing all the app features that use the network. If you are using an iPod touch, just disconnect from WiFi in order to test.

Dear Developer,

Your application, Card Counter, cannot be submitted to the App Store because it uses a standard ContactAdd button for an action that is not its intended purpose. Applications must adhere to the iPhone Human Interface Guidelines as outlined in iPhone SDK Agreement section 3.3.5.

The ContactAdd button is to be used to display a people picker to add a contact to an item. In your application, it is used to increase the count of the cards displayed, as seen in the screenshot attached. Implementing standard buttons to perform other tasks will lead to user confusion.

Please review the System-Provided Buttons and Icons section of the iPhone's Human Interface Guidelines here: *https://developer.apple.com/iphone/library/documentation/UserExperience/Conceptual/MobileHIG*

In order for your application to be reconsidered for the App Store, please resolve this issue and upload your new binary to iTunes Connect.

Regards,

iPhone Developer Program

I was using a button that contained a graphic similar to their ContactAd button. Although it made sense for my game, it was just too similar to their stock button. You need to make sure the buttons you use do not appear like the default stock buttons. I fixed this by buying a set of really professional-looking icons that were themed completely different from controls found in iOS.

My next rejection came when I updated my game to be a universal application to support the full screen of the iPad.

Dear Developer,

Thank you for submitting Card Counter to the App Store. We've reviewed your application and determined that we cannot post this version of your iPad application to the App Store. Applications must adhere to the iPad Human Interface Guidelines as outlined in the iPhone Developer Program License Agreement section 3.3.5.

The iPad Human Interface Guidelines state that an iPad application should be able to run in all orientations. Card Counter is only supporting one variant of the portrait orientation. While we understand there are certain applications that need to run in the portrait orientation, it would be appropriate to support both variants of this orientation in your application.

Please note that supporting all four orientations, each with unique launch images, provides the best user experience and is recommended. Please review the Aim to Support All Orientations section of the iPad's Human Interface Guidelines here:

*http://developer.apple.com/iphone/library/documentation/General
/Conceptual/iPadHIG/iPadHIG.pdf*

In order for your application to be reconsidered for the App Store,
please resolve this issue and upload your new binary to iTunes
Connect. Should you require technical assistance, you may use
one of your Technical Support Incidents included in your iPhone
Developer Program by sending an email to Apple Developer
Technical Support.

Sincerely,

App Review Team

This time the App Review Team got it wrong, as my game already supported
portrait and upside-down portrait orientations. I'm guessing the reviewer had
their screen orientation lock engaged when they reviewed the app. I responded to
the reviewer with a follow-up email and attached a screenshot of the game in the
middle of a screen rotation.

Dear App Review Team,

The version that we submitted supports both variants of portrait
mode for iPad. The iPhone version supports only one. Attached is a
screenshot of Card Counter when you rotate the iPad device to portrait upside down. As you can see it rotates to that orientation. Can
you please clarify the issue?

Thanks,

Todd

I received the following response:

Hello Todd,

Thank you for the clarification. We'll proceed with the review.

Sincerely,

App Review Team

Guess they don't always get it right, so it is nice they let you follow-up with an email. This next rejection was not for the game itself but for the application description of the game.

> Dear Todd,
>
> Thank you for submitting Tic Tac Blackjack Lite to the App Store. We've reviewed Tic Tac Blackjack Lite and determined that we cannot post this version of your iPhone application to the App Store because your application contains pricing information in the marketing text (Application Description / Release Notes). Providing specific pricing information in these locations may lead to user confusion because of pricing differences in countries. It would be appropriate to remove pricing information from these locations.
>
> Once the necessary modifications are completed, please let us know so we can proceed with the review.
>
> Regards,
>
> iPhone Developer Program

Never mention the price of your game in the application description. As I mentioned before, you can say "Free" or even "50% Off" but when you list a price it will cause the rest of the world to get confused since it wouldn't be in their local currency. iTunes shows the price in the Buy button in the user's local currency so there is no need to mention it. Here's another rejection received from the same game:

> Hello Todd,
>
> Your application, Tic Tac Blackjack Lite, cannot be posted to the App Store at this time because it does not achieve the core functionality described in your marketing materials, or release notes. Applications must adhere to the iPhone Human Interface Guidelines as outlined in the iPhone Developer Program License Agreement section 3.3.5.
>
> The release notes for Tic Tac Blackjack Lite state, "also allows you to start at any puzzle you want"; however, users can only choose from

the puzzles they have previously solved. This review was conducted on iPhone 3G running iPhone OS 3.0.1.

In order for your application to be reconsidered for the App Store, please resolve this issue and upload your new binary to iTunes Connect.

Should you require more assistance with resolving this issue, Apple Developer Technical Support is available to provide direct one-on-one support for discrete code-level questions. Please be sure to include any crash logs, screenshots, or steps to reproduce this issue in your request.

Regards,

iPhone Developer Program

I was kind of surprised that the reviewer actually took that hard of a look at my game. They were correct in that you couldn't start at any puzzle and you could only start at puzzles you previously solved. This was another simple fix that only required changing the release notes in the application description.

The next rejection comes from my poor use of icon images.

Dear Todd,

White Noise cannot be posted to the App Store because the small bundle icon does not match your large icon. This might be confusing to users.

iTunes Connect Users Guide, pg 27 C) Large Icon (512x512) The small (57x57) icon that you include inside the binary will be used on the home screen, and the App Store when viewed from the iPod touch and iPhone. The large icon will be used to feature your application on the iTunes App Store.

Please resolve this issue and upload a new binary and correct meta-data using iTunes Connect (*http://itunesconnect.apple.com/*)

Regards,

iPhone Developer Program

My large icon was slightly different from my smaller application icon. You should always design your icon to target the iTunes size of 512×512 and then downsize to all the other required dimensions for use in the application. It makes sense that users will expect to see the same icon while using both the desktop version of iTunes and the device version of the App Store. The next rejection was upsetting, in that this was a highly requested feature by customers of my application. It just wasn't permitted by Apple:

> Dear Mr. Moore,
>
> Thank you for submitting White Noise to the App Store. Unfortunately it cannot be added to the App Store because it is using a private API. Use of non-public APIs, which as outlined in the iPhone Developer Program License Agreement section 3.3.1 is prohibited:
>
> "3.3.1 Applications may only use Documented APIs in the manner prescribed by Apple and must not use or call any private APIs."
>
> The non-public API that is included in your application is terminate.
>
> In order for your application to be reconsidered for the App Store, please resolve this issue and upload your new binary to iTunes Connect.
>
> Please respond to this email once you have resubmitted your binary and we will expedite your review.
>
> Regards,
>
> iPhone Developer Program

My application included a feature to allow closing of the application automatically using a timer, which could help save battery life. This was accomplished by calling **terminate** on the application object. It turns out this method was not documented and not permitted. In the end, I solved it by calling the C-based **exit** function, which is not the ideal way to implement this because it doesn't gracefully do a proper application shutdown, however it is on the list of permitted functions. I doubt you will need to ever do this in a game but I mention it so that you are aware that you cannot call undocumented methods.

Hello Todd,

Your application, White Noise Lite cannot be posted to the App Store at this time because it is a feature-limited version. Free or "Lite" versions are acceptable, however the application must be fully functional and cannot reference features that are not implemented. In White Noise Lite, multiple sound options contained under Sound Catalog, the Pitch control feature in Sound Settings, and Timer Settings are not available.

Please upload a new binary and correct metadata using iTunes Connect (*http://itunesconnect.apple.com/*).

Best regards,

iPhone Application Review Team

I had controls that were disabled on the screen with a note saying upgrade to enable this functionality. This is not permitted. You can have an upgrade page within your application to promote your full version but you can't show features that are disabled within the app itself. I've seen many games that were approved that push the boundaries of this, such as having buttons that reference new levels but when clicked say you need to upgrade. I've seen levels in extremely popular games that say "coming soon," which is clearly referencing missing implementation. I'm assuming games are given more leniency with this rule rather than standard applications such as my White Noise app.

My most recent rejection comes from the Paddles game created in this book. This is more of an automated message and it is also the rejection I've seen the most:

Dear Developer,

We have discovered one or more issues with your recent binary submission for "Paddles". The following issues will need to be corrected in order for your application to proceed to review:

Invalid Signature - Make sure you have signed your application with a distribution certificate, not an ad hoc certificate or a development certificate. Verify that the code signing settings in Xcode are correct at the target level (which override any values at the

project level). Additionally, make sure the bundle you are uploading was built using a Release target in Xcode, not a Simulator target. If you are certain your code signing settings are correct, choose
"Clean All" in Xcode, delete the "build" directory in the Finder, and
rebuild your release target.

Once you have corrected these issues, go to the app's version
details page (found in the Manage Your Applications module of
iTunes Connect) and click Ready to Submit Binary. Proceed through
the submission process until the app's status is Waiting for Upload.
You can then use Application Loader to upload the corrected
binary.

Regards,

The iTunes Store Team

The description on how to fix this problem seems to solve it every time. The
Xcode project settings are usually always to blame here. If you ever see this message, and I'm assuming you will, make sure you are using the correct certificate
for App Store distribution specified in the application target. I also recommend
doing a clean build of the application before submitting again.

Those are just a few of the many rejections I have received over the years. There
are a lot of guidelines to follow and they do change over time so you will probably
discover many more going forward. Hopefully now that you have seen a few of
my rejections you won't feel too bad if it happens to you.

App Marketing and Sales

There are numerous ways to market your application and I recommend you try them all out to get a feel for what works for you. The first thing you need to know is a strategy of "submit it and they will come" is probably not going to work. When I submitted my first game there were fewer than 1,000 apps in the store so it was much easier to get noticed. Now that there are over a half million applications you will have to put forth some effort in order to get noticed.

I have been fortunate to have had many of my applications featured by the iTunes staff or reviewed in major newspapers and online blogs. This kind of exposure can have a huge impact on the success and ranking of your app. I'll cover a few websites that I recommend that can help promote and advertise your application. I'll also cover how to track your app's ranking and sales. Hopefully you will find success in implementing some or all of these strategies.

The first thing you need is a link to your application in the iTunes App Store. You can either log in to iTunes Connect and get the link from the product page or just fire up iTunes and right-click on your icon and copy the link. For example, my most popular game, Card Counter, has the following link:

http://itunes.apple.com/us/app/card-counter/id293742180?mt=8

Clicking on that link will bring up a preview of the application in the web browser, and if iTunes is installed it will bring up the listing and allow for immediate purchase. It also works on the mobile device, too. You will want to always include this link for every place that you post about your application.

There are other ways to launch into the iTunes store using search parameters. For example, if I wanted to link to all my published applications in the App Store, I could use the following:

http://itunes.com/apps/toddmoore

That will bring up all the apps listed under my name. If I wanted to bring up a specific application such as the Paddles game (shown in Figure 7-4), I could use the following link:

http://itunes.com/apps/toddmoore/paddles

You can also just search for the application name without the company specified but I do not recommend it, as it could bring up other applications with similar names that are not your own. The last thing you want to do is promote someone else's app, so always include your company identifier with the search link.

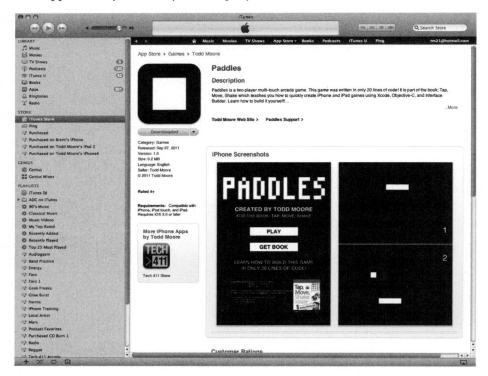

Figure 7-4. Launching iTunes to a specific application

The Social Network

The first places to start promoting your application is on email, Facebook, Twitter, and Google+. Hopefully you already have signed up for all the social networks, but if not it is time to join in on the fun. Friends and family will always download your new game, especially if it is your first venture into the App Store. They probably will grow tired of hearing about your new app after releasing over 30 of them (like I have) but initially they will be your best customers. Every download helps and hopefully if they like it they will leave you a nice review.

I've been asked before if you should create a Facebook page for each app you release. I find it best to just create one single company page. For example, I use *www.facebook.com/tmsoft* as my company page and I promote all my applications there. I also have a Twitter account under @tmsoft (*http://twitter.com/tmsoft*), which is linked to my Facebook page so both accounts get updated at the same time. You could set up different accounts and pages for each application you create but I find it best to keep your followers up-to-date with a single Facebook page and Twitter account. This also has the benefit of letting you cross-promote to existing customers when new apps come out.

The iTunes Feature

Nothing listed here works better than getting your game featured in the iTunes App Store. Every week Apple will feature a new batch of apps and games. This can really drive a ton of downloads and it doesn't cost a thing. I have been fortunate to have a couple of my apps and games featured, but please know that there is no way to make sure this happens. I can however tell you a few general guidelines that will help better position yourself for selection.

Apple wants you to make their platform look great. Period. Your game needs to have awesome graphics, sounds, and music. They also like when you use the latest iOS features. When the iPad first came out, I updated Glow Burst as a universal application and submitted it before the iPad was available for purchase. It was featured in both the iPhone and iPad App Store (shown in Figure 7-5). When the iPhone 4 came out, I updated it again to support the Retina display. It was also featured again. When Game Center came out, I quickly updated it to support leaderboards and achievements. It was featured yet again. Either someone over there really liked my game or they really appreciated my usage of the latest features of iOS. I'm guessing it was a little of both.

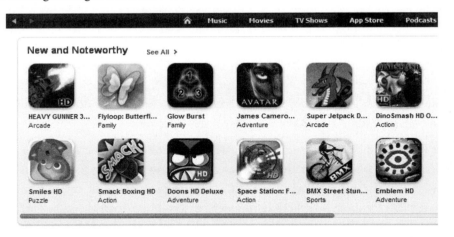

Figure 7-5. Glow Burst featured in iTunes next to Avatar

I created another game called Lift Off to help promote my friend's song that was also named Lift Off. I feel strongly that combining good music with your game is almost a requirement to getting featured. If you know some independent artists that have their music in iTunes then you should definitely ask them if you can use it, especially if it fits the game. It helps promote their music (links to songs work the same as apps in iTunes) and helps you by making your game more unique. The Lift Off game was featured in iTunes under the Game section.

It feels great to see your application featured by Apple and I hope you get to experience it. It means you did something right. It's like getting a pat on the back for a job well done. If it happens to you, make sure to promote the fact in both your application description, website, and everywhere else your app is mentioned.

Free Web Reviews

Now that your application has been approved and is available for download, it is time to market it. The first website you should check out is *http://www.gotoats. org/*—which has a listing of iPhone app and game review sites that "uphold proper editorial ethics and standards." In short, these sites do not have paid reviews. That means the reviews will be honest and they will never try to get you to pay for your app to be reviewed. That also means they may not care to review your game, but you should always reach out and let everyone on the list know about your new release. A free review of your game will certainly drive additional downloads.

One of the best websites for game reviews is *http://toucharcade.com/*. If your game gets reviewed there it will certainly drive a ton of downloads. Even posting about your game in the forums is a great way to get your game some attention. Make sure to create an account and use their forums. You might even be able to get some feedback from gamers, especially if you give a few promo codes.

If you are charging money for your app, you can use promotional codes to give users the ability to download a free copy. Promotional codes can be retrieved from the iTunes Connect website. You get 50 codes per application update and they expire after 30 days from when you retrieve them. This is a fantastic way to give web reviewers a free copy, and hopefully if they like your game they will review your app. If somebody wants to write about your app, you should always give them a free copy. The more people that write about your game the better, and the more links you can get to the iTunes store or your own website will help raise your PageRank in Google.

One thing to know is if someone uses a promo code then they will not be able to leave a review on iTunes. Promo code downloads also do not contribute to your application ranking. I recommend saving your promo codes for people that might give you a web review or provide you with direct feedback about the game.

The Lite Version

A lite version is a fantastic way to promote the full version of your app. It's basically free marketing. It allows potential customers to try out your game and you can even earn additional money by using services such as iAd or AdMob to display ads within your game. I recommend taking a few features out of your game in order to give customers a reason to upgrade. For example, one of my most featured games on iTunes was Glow Burst, and I made sure to create a lite version to help promote it. The lite version only has one level of difficulty and includes advertising on the main screen. It has direct links to purchase the full version in the App Store.

The lite version does a lot to promote your application. First, you will get more downloads because it is free. People that play and like your game might tell others about it and then they can download it, too. You can earn money off the free app by using an ad network. I recommend using an ad aggregator such as AdWhirl (*https://www.adwhirl.com/*) so you can control which ad network you want to use at any point. This allows you to rotate between networks, which helps to make sure you get higher fill rates. You can also run your own house ads using AdWhirl, so it's easy to cross-promote other apps and games you create.

If you want to run your own advertising campaign, one thing that is great about AdMob is if you have made money by being an ad publisher, you can transfer money into your advertising account. The nice thing about this approach is they usually give a bonus of around 20% when you do the transfer. This is a good way to get more mileage out of your advertising dollars. You can always fund the account from a bank account if you haven't earned enough money from the publisher side. AdMob also is really easy to get set up and running. I'll talk more about running paid ad campaigns next.

Paid Advertising

Who are the best people to advertise your new iPhone game to? Obviously the people that have an iPhone and download and use apps. It is much better to advertise within other iPhone apps then on a regular website or within search results using Google AdSense. This of course will cost money, and if that's okay then I recommend using a service like AdMob. You can target the people that have iPhones or iPads, specific iOS versions, and even down to the country or city. Running ad campaigns using this kind of targetting is the best use of your funds. If you have enough money to run a decent campaign then this is the easiest way to get a lot of downloads, especially if the game is free. I do not recommend advertising paid apps. You will have a much better success rate if you pay to advertise a free version of your game. And then, once downloaded, the free version can be used to drive paid downloads of the full version.

AdMob offers a pay-per-click model, which means you pay whenever somebody clicks on the ad. The ad will take the person to the App Store listing of your application. This doesn't mean you will get a download, as they might decide against downloading it. The best ratio I've ever experienced was 1 out of 4 clicks resulted in a download. You just can't do much better than 25% of all clicks resulting in a download. I was paying $0.05 a click and $.20 a download for my free app. These results are the absolute best results that I have ever seen and it happened only after running and tweaking numerous ad campaigns. These results were so good, in fact, that it caught the attention of AdMob and we did a case study together on the campaign. I will cover the strategy I use when I advertise later, but first I need to go over a few advertising terms you will need to know in order to understand what you are paying for and how to track the success of your marketing campaign.

- Ad: The ad usually includes a single image of a specific size, such as 320×48 or a 38×38 icon with one line of text. The icon with text ad has a lower cost, but the text is limited to 35 characters so you might have to get a little creative to get your point across. There is a single link that usually launches off the App Store or other web page. It is best to direct customers right to your application in the App Store so it only takes one more click to download.

- Bid: How much are you willing to pay for someone who clicks on your ad? That is your bid price, and usually you will accept the minimum allowed by the ad network. The minimum bid will change based on the type of ad you run and how targeted the campaign is. You usually will not raise the bid higher than the minimum unless you notice your ad is not running. This happens when people have outbid you and their ad gets priority. I have only had to raise my minimum bid between Christmas and New Years, as there are a lot of companies taking out advertising and making higher bids so their inventory runs. All other times I have not seen an issue using the minimum bid.

- Impressions: This is the number of times your ad has been displayed. A popular metric is called CPM, which is cost per thousand impressions. Even though you are paying for clicks, this calculation lets you know how much you are paying every time you ad is viewed 1,000 times. Some ad vendors allow you to pay for impressions but most of the mobile ad networks typically only support paying for clicks.

- Clicks: The amount you pay for clicks is known as CPC, or cost per click. You specify how much you are willing to pay for a click in the bid price.

- CTR: Click through rate is the ratio between impressions and how many times a person clicks on the ad.

- Cost: This is total amount you are paying across all your campaigns. Generally, you set a daily limit on how much you are willing to spend, so if you had $3,000 to spend on your ad campaign you could divide that up over a number of days.

- Downloads: This is the number of downloads you have gotten from your campaign. You will have to add some tracking code into your application in order to get this statistic. I highly recommend you do this because without this metric you really don't know how your campaign is doing. At the end of the day, you want downloads. And just getting the number of clicks your ad has received does not paint the whole story.

- Conversion Rate: This is the ratio between clicks and downloads. Obviously you want this to be as high as possible.

- Cost/Download: This is the most important metric. How much are you paying per download? On average you will probably be paying around $1 per download. I've seen campaigns cost as much as $20 for a single download and that is just horrible. You are getting too many clicks and not enough downloads if that happens. I usually stop running an ad campaign that costs more than a dollar per download.

Let's take an actual example that will hopefully help you understand the terms mentioned above. I ran a campaign that targeted iPhone users in the United States, which had a minimum bid or CPC of 5 cents. This particular campaign resulted in about one million impressions. That means my ad was displayed one million times to iPhone users in the United States. I had roughly 6,000 clicks on my ad, which cost me $300. Because I had conversion tracking put into my application, I could get the total number of downloads—which was about 250. This gave a conversion rate that was around 4%. So 4% of the clicks would result in a download. Or if you want to look at it another way, 96% of the clicks were wasted money. Get used to that. The most important metric is what I was paying per download, which ended up being $1.20. That's not very good for a free application so I ended stopping that campaign and going with others that were producing better results.

I recommend always creating multiple ad campaigns and always put download tracking into your application before starting a campaign. Each of your ads should have a different message. You don't get a lot of space if you're putting in a 35 character message, but in advertising less is usually more. Nobody wants to read a lot of text. Try to catch the users attention. Make them want to click and see what your app is all about. You will notice all of the ad campaigns you create will always perform differently. I keep a close eye on the performance of my campaigns and shut down ones that are performing poorly before too much money is spent.

I typically create about 10 different ads and test them out over time to see which perform better. The more ads you create, the better chance of success you will have. Remember that app rankings on iTunes are country specific. If you are trying to get a higher rank in a specific country, you should create campaigns that target those regions. I typically always target the United States, as that has typically been the biggest source of revenue for my apps.

Tracking Sales & Ranks

iTunes Connect offers sales data for applications on the iOS and Mac App Stores, as well as advertising profits using iAd. There is also a mobile application you can download from iTunes Connect that gives you access to the data. I have a couple other services I use that retrieve and provide reports on the sales and rank data.

I recommend App Annie (*http://www.AppAnnie.com*) for tracking your application ranks. As shown in Figure 7-6, App Annie is displaying historic ranking data for Glow Burst when it was featured and became the #1 Kids game on the iPad. You can also use this service to track sales and rankings together. I signed up for this service because they send you a daily email with sales numbers, application ranks, and new customer reviews. It really is one of the best services around.

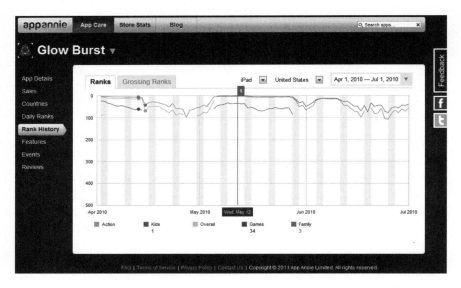

Figure 7-6. App Annie graphs historic app rankings

If you don't feel comfortable letting a third party have access to your sales data and would rather download it locally to your computer, then I recommend using AppViz by IdeaSwarm (*http://www.ideaswarm.com/*) for that purpose. It's a great Mac application that downloads sales data for both the iOS and Mac App Store. It also includes iAd profits, application reviews, and app rankings. I use this application in addition to the App Annie website, so I have a local copy of all my sales data.

Conclusion

I hope you have enjoyed this adventure to the App Store as much as I enjoyed putting this book together. There is much to know in this new world of mobile applications and hopefully you were able to get a few gems out of this book. I encourage you to write all your ideas for games and apps down in a document as they come to you. New game ideas constantly come to me and there is no way I could implement them all. But I write them all down and when I do get free time, I like to pick one and run with it. Make sure to take on projects that you feel you can actually accomplish and of course make sure it's an idea that would be approved by Apple.

I covered a lot of ground here and hopefully you now have the skills to create code, graphics, and sounds to give your new game the best shot at success. Do not get discouraged if you don't get featured on iTunes right out of the gate. It takes time and it's a continuous learning process. I would love to see your creations so please let me know when your game becomes available for download. The best place to contact me is at my website (*http://toddmoore.com/*) or on Twitter @toddmoore (*http://twitter.com/toddmoore*). Good luck to you and I hope you find success in the App Store.

A

AAC format, 162
ad aggregators, 240
AdMob service, 239, 240
Adobe graphics products, 90–91
advertising, paid, 240–243
AdWhirl.com website, 240
afconvert tool, 162
.aif files, 81, 161
Air Hockey game
    application integration, 116–121
    bitmap format and, 91
    computer player difficulty levels,
        205–211
    computer player menu, 173–183
    creating application icons, 114–116
    designing computer player, 183–204
    Interface Builder and, 118–121
    making button images, 110–112
    making paddle image, 102–116
    making puck image, 97–102
    making table image, 106–110
    recording sounds, 166–167
    reviewing game images, 113
    simulator operations, 121
airplane mode, 226
alertView:didDismissWithButtonIndex
        method, 182
animation
    in Air Hockey game, 139–157
    in Paddles game, 59–62
AppAnnie.com website, 243
App ID, 219
App Info file, 42
Apple Developer website, 1
Apple ID, 1
application description, 216–217
applicationDidBecomeActive method,
        21, 25, 77
applicationDidEnterBackground meth-
        od, 21

application:didFinishLaunchingWithOpt
        ions method, 21, 25
application icons, 114–116, 231–232
application names, 216, 218
applications. *See* building and running
        applications
application states, 19–25, 187
applicationWillEnterForeground meth-
        od, 21
applicationWillResignActive method,
        22, 77
applicationWillTerminate method, 22
App Ocean (app), 165
App Store
    application review, 226–234
    archiving apps, 224–225
    creating app description/keywords,
        216–218
    featuring new apps/games, 237–238
    lite version, 239
    marketing applications, 235–244
    screenshots of apps, 213–215
    submitting meta to iTunes Connect,
        218–223
    Top Grossing category, 220
    Top Paid category, 220
    tracking sales/ranking, 243
AppViz application, 244
arc4random() function, 35, 59
Assistant option (Editor submenu/View
        menu), 30
atan2 function, 129
Atari Home Pong console, 39
Attributes Inspector
    about, 26–27
    computer player example, 173
    depicted, 45
    opening, 43
Audacity tool, 167–171
audio. *See* sounds
AudioServicesCreateSystemSoundID
        method, 84

AudioServicesPlaySystemSound function, 85, 161
AudioToolbox framework, 82–83
automatic snapshots, 118
Autorelease memory pool, 20
AVAudioPlayer class, 162

B

background images, creating, 106–116
backwards compatibility for applications, 95
bitmap graphics format
about, 91
exporting vector format in, 92
scaling images and, 91–93
transparency support, 93
breakpoint navigator, 8, 10
breakpoints, adding/deleting, 11
building and running applications. *See also* Air Hockey game; Paddles game
application integration, 116–121
application states, 19–25
backwards compatibility, 95
device considerations, 16–17
game logic, 34–37
iOS version considerations, 16, 41
simulator operations, 14–16
Bundle ID (apps), 219
buttons
computer player example, 174–176
creating, 110–121
design considerations, 228

C

.caf files, 81, 161
Card Counter (app), xii, 226–229, 235
CGPointMake function, 54
CGPoint structure, 54
CGRectIntersectsRect structure, 63
CGRectMake function, 63

CGRect structure, 63
Click Through Rate (CTR), 242
Code Completion feature, 10
collision detection
about, 63–65
puck physics, 139–157
sounds for, 81
color codes, hexadecimal, 98, 102
Command-F keyboard shortcut, 168
Command-R keyboard shortcut, 14
Command-Shift-4 keyboard shortcut, 214
compressed formats, 162–163
computer player
computer player menu, 173–183
creating difficulty levels for, 205–211
defensive state and, 189–194
designing from scratch, 183–204
offensive strategy and, 194–204
Connection Inspector, 26
connections
creating, 30–34
laying out game pieces, 47–49
Control-click keyboard shortcut, 31
Control-Space keyboard shortcut, 10
cos function, 129
CPC (cost per click), 242
Creative Commons Sample Plus license, 163
CTR (Click Through Rate), 242

D

dealloc method
Air Hockey game, 125, 132–133
Paddles game, 49, 144
debug area (Xcode interface), 13, 51
debug navigator, 8, 9
decoding compressed formats, 162–163
defensive state (computer player), 189–194
delegates, defined, 20
Deployment Target, configuring, 41–42

developers, registering, 1

Device option (Hardware menu), 15

devices

  orientation considerations, 41, 136–137, 228

  registering for development, 16–17

  removing status bar display, 42

  screenshots of apps, 213–215

  shake gesture and, 78–81

  silent mode, 87

  typical screen sizes, 94

difficulty levels for games

  for computer player, 205–211

  increasing, 74–75

digital recordings, 160

direction, tracking, 59–61

displaying messages in Paddle game, 69–71

display resolution, 94–96, 215

distance formula calculation, 127–128

distortion (sound), 165

downloading sounds, 163–171

DropBox iPhone app, 215

drop shadows, 100, 104, 108

Duplicate option (File menu), 117

E

editing sounds, 167–171

editor area (Xcode interface)

  about, 10–12

  Code Completion feature, 10

  Fix-it feature, 11

  opening files in, 8

Editor menu, 47

Editor segment control, 30

Ellipse tool (Adobe Fireworks), 97–98, 103, 106

Empty Application template, 6

ending score in Paddles game, 72–74

error conditions, displaying, 227

EULA (End User License Agreement), 222

exporting graphics files, 92, 101

F

fabs() function, 63

fading out audio, 170

File Inspector, 13

File menu

  Duplicate option, 117

  New submenu, 4, 40

filename convention, 95–96

filter bar

  about, 8

  displaying symbols, 9

Fit Canvas button, 99–100

Fix-it feature, 11

flat view (symbol navigator), 9

focus ribbon, 11–12

Font button, 28

freesound.org website, 163

G

GameAppDelegate.h file, 12, 18

GameAppDelegate.m file, 18, 20

Game-Info.plist file, 19

game layout and logic

  connections, 47–49

  defensive state for computer player, 189–194

  game elements, xiii

  Interface Builder support, 43–47

  for math problem, 34–37

  offensive strategy for computer player, 194–204

  paddle physics, 123–139

  puck physics, 139–157

Game-Prefix.pch file, 19

GameViewController.h file, 18, 30

GameViewController.m file, 18, 23

GameViewController.xib file, 18, 26

Garage Band tool, 163

Gimp program, 90

Glow Burst (app), 164, 237–238

Google AdWords, 217

gotoats.org website, 238

gradients, changing, 98–99, 112
graphics in games. *See also* Air Hockey
    game
  application integration, 116–121
  bitmaps and vectors, 91–93
  image formats, 93
  importance of, 89
  options for, 89–90
  retina display technology, 94–96
  tools to create, 90–91
gutter, defined, 11

H

Hardware menu
  Device option, 15, 121
  Home Button option, 15
  Lock option, 15
  Rotate Left | Right option, 15
  Shake Gesture option, 15
  Version option, 15
hexadecimal color codes, 98, 102
hierarchical view (symbol navigator), 9
home button, 15, 77, 213
Human Interface Guidelines (Apple), 226

I

iAd service, 239, 243
icons, application, 114–116, 231–232
IdeaSwarm.com website, 244
Identity Inspector, 26
IMA/ADPCM (IMA4) format, 81, 161–162
image formats
  about, 93
  best practices, 92
  Interface Builder and, 118–121
Image Preview screen (Adobe
    Fireworks), 102, 109
initWithView method, 125–126
Inkscape tool, 90
inspectors, choosing from, 43. *See*
    also specific inspectors

installing Xcode, 2–3
Interface Builder
  about, 26–29
  dragging images into, 118–121
  laying out game pieces, 43–47
  WYSIWYG editor, 43
intValue method, 36, 67
iOS Dev Center program, 1
iOS Provisioning Portal, 219
iOS Simulator menu, 16
iPhone (Retina) option (Device sub-
    menu/Hardware menu), 121
iPhoto software, 215
issue navigator, 8, 9
iTunes App Store. *See* App Store
iTunes Connect
  Add New App button, 218
  entering credentials, 224
  Manage Your Applications, 218
  promotional codes, 239
  submitting meta to, 218–223
  tracking sales/ranking, 243
  uploading photos to, 215

J

JPEG format, 93

K

keyboard shortcuts. *See* specific key-
    board shortcuts
keywords for apps, 217–218

L

labels, positioning, 28
Lift Off (app), 238
lite version (apps), 239
locationInView method, 53
Lock option (Hardware menu), 15
log navigator, 8, 10
lossy formats, 93, 167

M

main.m file, 19–20
marketing applications, 235–244
master copy (sound recordings), 167
Master-Detail Application template, 5
math problem, game logic for, 34–37
Media library, 118
memory leaks, 33
messages, displaying, 69–71
motionBegan method, 79–80
motionCancelled method, 79
motionEnded method, 79–80
motion events, 78–81
MP3 format, 162, 167
multipleTouchEnabled property, 52
multi-touch functionality
    about, 49–50
    enabling, 51–53
    issues when implementing, 55–56
    methods of, 50–51
    moving paddles, 53–55
    tracking touch objects, 56–59
musicloops.com website, 164

N

Nash, Courtney, 135, 165
Navigation-based Application template, 5
navigator area (Xcode interface), 8–10
New Project option (New submenu/File
        menu), 4, 40
New Referencing Outlet, 31
nfoPlist.strings file, 19
normalizing sounds, 165, 170
NSLog function, 19–20, 22
NSObject class, 140
NSString class
    displaying symbols, 9
    intValue method, 36, 67
    stringWithFormat method, 35
    text property, 36
NSTimer object, 61

O

Object Library
    about, 26, 45
    depicted, 45
offensive strategy (computer player),
        194–204
onPlay method, 176–177
OpenAL (Open Audio Library), 164
OpenGL Game template, 5
Option-Command-0 keyboard shortcut,
        12
Organizer application, 16
orientation, device
    app design considerations, 41, 228
    touch point tool, 136–137
Outline View, 46

P

paddles
    in Air Hockey game, 102–116
    collision detection, 75
    computer player example, 183–186
    increasing game difficulty via, 74–75
    moving, 53–55
    paddle physics, 123–139
Paddles game
    animation in, 59–62
    collision detection, 63–65, 81
    depicted, 39
    displaying messages in, 69–71
    ending score, 72–74
    increasing difficulty of, 74–75
    laying out game pieces, 43–49
    multi-touch functionality, 49–59
    pause/resume logic in, 76–77
    project creation, 40–43
    scoring functionality, 65–69
    shake gesture in, 78–81
    sounds in, 81–87
paid advertising (apps), 240–243
partnersinrhyme.com website, 164
pause/resume logic in Paddles game, 76–77

pay-per-click advertising, 241
PCM format, 81, 161–162, 167
personal profiles, creating, 1
placeholder text in text fields, 28
PNG format, 93–94, 101
Polygon tool (Adobe Fireworks), 98
Pong game. *See* Paddles game
pricing information for apps, 217, 220, 230
printf function, 19, 35
project creation
    about, 4, 6–7, 40
    in Air Hockey game, 117
    App Info file, 42
    target settings, 41–42
project navigator
    opening, 8
    Supporting Files group, 19
project templates
    Empty Application, 6
    Master-Detail Application, 5
    OpenGL Game, 5
    Page-based Application, 5
    Single View Application, 6, 18, 40
    Tabbed Application, 5
    Utility Application, 5
promotional codes, 239
pucks
    in Air Hockey game, 97–102
    animating in Paddles game, 59–62
    increasing game difficulty via, 74–75
    puck physics, 139–157

Q

Quick Help, 13

R

rand() function, 35
random() function, 35
random number generation, 35, 188

Realistic iPhone Game Development video series, 135
recording sounds, 164–167
Rectangle tool (Adobe Fireworks), 98, 106
registering
    Apple developers, 1
    application names, 218
    devices for developing, 17
Release mode, 224
Reset Content and Settings option (iOS Simulator menu), 16
reset function, 60–62, 127
retina display
    about, 94–96
    Air Hockey game, 121
    screenshots of apps and, 215
RGB color code, 98
rollbacks to project snapshots, 118
Rotate Left | Right option (Hardware menu), 15
Rounded Rect vector tool, 111
running applications. *See* building and running applications

S

sample format, 161
sample rate, 160–161
scaling images, 91–93, 101
scoring
    about, 65–69
    ending score, 72–74
    puck physics, 139–157
screen lock button, 213
screen refresh rate, 61
screen resolution, 94–96, 215
screenshots of apps, 213–215
search navigator, 8, 9
secondary editor, enabling, 30
Send to Back option (Arrangement sub-menu/Editor menu), 47
shake gesture in Paddles game, 78–81

Shake Gesture option (Hardware menu), 15

Show Debug Area option (View menu), 13, 51

Show | Hide Utilities option (Utilities submenu/View menu), 12

silent mode, 87

simulator
about, 14–37
for Air Hockey game, 121
taking screenshots with, 214

sin function, 129

Single View Application template
about, 6
selecting, 40
skeleton files included, 18

Size Inspector
about, 26
computer player example, 173
depicted, 46

SKU Number (apps), 219

snapshots, automatic, 118

social networking, 237–238

sounds
about, 159
creating, 163
digital recordings and, 160
downloading, 163–171
editing, 167–171
file formats supported, 161–163
normalizing, 165, 170
playing different effects, 81–87
recording, 164–167

speed
calculating maximum, 128
image formats and, 93
tracking in Paddles game, 59–61

status bar
removing, 42
touch handling and, 136–137

storing artwork, 101

stringWithFormat method, 35

submit function, 35

Supporting Files folder, 42

Supporting Files group (project navigator), 19

suspended state, 33, 77

symbol navigator, 8, 9

@synthesize declaration, 125

System Audio Services, 81

T

Tabbed Application template, 5

tag property, 36, 176

target settings
about, 41–42
accessing, 40

templates, project. *See* project templates

text fields
placeholder text in, 28
using for input, 27

text property, 36

Text tool (Adobe Fireworks), 108

Top Grossing category (App Store), 220

Top Paid category (App Store), 220

toucharcade.com website, 239

touchesBegan method
about, 50
Air Hockey game example, 132
computer player example, 185
enabling touches, 53
moving paddles, 54
tracking touch objects, 56–57

touchesCancelled method
about, 50
tracking touch objets, 59

touchesEnded method
about, 50
Air Hockey game example, 134
tracking touch objects, 58

touchesMoved method
about, 50
Air Hockey game example, 133
moving paddles, 54
tracking touch objects, 57

touch functionality. *See* multi-touch functionality
tracking direction and speed, 59–61
transparency, defined, 93

U

UIAlertView class
  displaying messages, 69–71
  tag property, 36
UIApplicationDelegate protocol, 13
UIApplicationMain function, 20
UIButton class, 181
UIImageView object, 118
UIScreen object, 95
UITouch object
  locationInView method, 53
  multi-touch functionality and, 52–53
  paddle physics and, 131
  storing, 132
UIView class
  Air Hockey game example, 126
  collision detection, 63
  math problem example, 35
  Paddles game example, 48
UIViewController class, 47, 173
UIWindow object, 95
USB dock connector, 16
Use for Development button, 16
Utilities submenu (View menu)
  Attributes Inspector option, 43
  Object Library option, 26
  Show | Hide Utilities option, 12
Utility Application template, 5
utility area (Xcode interface)
  about, 12–13
  depicted, 45
  displaying, 12
  hiding, 12

V

validating applications, 224
vector graphics format
  about, 91
  exporting into bitmap format, 92
  scaling images and, 91–93
version considerations
  filename conventions and, 96
  iOS environment, 16, 41
Version Number (apps), 220
Version option (Hardware menu), 15
viewDidAppear function, 37
viewDidLoad function
  about, 33, 62
  Air Hockey game, 130
  computer player example, 211
  displaying messages, 71
  loading sounds, 84
  modifying, 35
  Paddles game, 151–152
viewDidUnload function
  Air Hockey game example, 132
  math problem example, 33
  Paddles game example, 49
viewDidUnload method
  math problem example, 33
View menu
  displaying Xcode interface areas, 7
  Editor submenu, 30
  Show Debug Area option, 13, 51
  Utilities submenu
    Attributes Inspector option, 43
    Object Library option, 26
    Show | Hide Utilities option, 12
View object, 45

W

.wav files, 81, 161
web reviews, 238
White Noise (app), xii, 231–233

X

Xcode
  application states, 19–25
  building and running applications,
        14–17
  code structure, 18–19
  creating connections, 30–34
  developer registration, 1
  game logic, 34–37
  installing, 2–3
  Interface Builder, 26–29
  launching, 4
  project types, 5–7
Xcode interface
  about, 7
  debug area, 13, 51
  editor area, 10–12
  navigator area, 8–10
  utility area, 12–13, 45

R75680